Everyday *Fancy*

Everyday *Fancy*

65 Easy, Elegant Recipes
for Meals, Snacks,
Sweets, *and* Drinks

COURTNEY LAPRESI

edited by Leda Scheintaub

photographs by Jennifer May

Stewart, Tabori & Chang | New York

Published in 2015 by Stewart, Tabori & Chang

An imprint of ABRAMS

Library of Congress Control Number: 2014952819

ISBN: 978-1-61769-150-8

Editor: Samantha Weiner
Designer: Danielle Young
Production Manager: True Sims

Food Stylist: Erin McDowell
Prop Stylist: Barbara Fritz

The text of this book was composed in Proxima Nova, Archer, and A Gentle Touch.

Printed and bound in the United States

10 9 8 7 6 5 4 3 2 1

 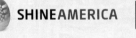

SHINE AMERICA   FOX™ Fox and its related entities. All rights reserved.   MasterChef   SHINE GROUP

Stewart, Tabori & Chang books are available at special discounts when purchased in quantity for premiums and promotions as well as fundraising or educational use. Special editions can also be created to specification. For details, contact specialsales@abramsbooks.com or the address below.

ABRAMS
THE ART OF BOOKS SINCE 1949

115 West 18th Street
New York, NY 10011
www.abramsbooks.com

DEDICATION

To the ones I love:

My mom, Lisa

My dad, Dennis

My brothers, Colby, Connor, and Cooper

My sister, Colette

And to Christina, who reminded me to "show up."

Contents

Foreword

Courtney Lapresi's journey is a wonderful example of what can be accomplished when genuine talent is combined with tenacity and an unwavering belief in oneself. For most of us, it's often the latter that is the most difficult to achieve, but Courtney held on to her faith in herself and her abilities, even under the most trying circumstances.

When Courtney first arrived in the *MasterChef* kitchen, my initial perception was one of much uncertainty. I honestly wasn't sure what to make of her. She was polite, chipper, and clearly confident, and I was curious to see if she actually had the culinary savoir faire to back up her bravado.

It quickly became quite clear that this young lady could cook and fragile, she certainly wasn't. Rarely making any missteps, Courtney maintained her place atop the *MasterChef* competition through to her victory in the finale. There wasn't a challenge she shied away from. Nothing we threw at her scared her. She was the one contestant to beat from the start and everyone knew it.

It isn't easy to pack up your life—literally overnight—and leave all that is comforting and familiar. Huge personal sacrifices are made each year by all our amateur cooks. They spend time away from their loved ones, give up their income—and in some cases their jobs—all while dealing with the pressure of a fierce, high-stakes competition. It is enough to break even the most grounded individuals. In all the past seasons of both *MasterChef USA* and *MasterChef Italia*, there have only been a few others who have handled the rigors with the grace and resilience shown by Courtney.

Like Courtney, I too found myself in my early twenties in a lucrative, albeit soul-sucking, career from which I could see no real prospect of happiness on the horizon. I was torn between an innate desire for financial security and a need to follow my heart, and it took a great deal of courage to leave my job on Wall Street and take a chance on a notoriously difficult industry racked with failure.

If you are going to put all your eggs in one basket, the restaurant industry is far from your safest bet. Savvy and much tougher than she may appear, Courtney is well aware of this—she is nobody's fool—but she chose to pursue her passion regardless. For Courtney, it proved to be a risk worth taking.

One of the youngest to win the *MasterChef* competition, Courtney possesses the strength, smarts, and desire to make a name for herself in the competitive world of food and wine, and I believe we will see great things from this resilient and bright gal from Philly.

A delightful collection of cookery featuring beloved classics as well as sophisticated twists on some favorite staples, *Everyday Fancy* is an approachable yet elegant must-have addition to every kitchen. From the feared croquembouche to old favorites such as homemade peanut butter and scones, Courtney has compiled a practical go-to manual for an array of meal options achievable for every home cook.

Buon appetito!

—Joe Bastianich

Introduction

When I chose to audition for *MasterChef*, I didn't tell anyone where I was going.

I had been a fan of the show for a few years, and I watched, enchanted, as home cooks were transformed into chefs. As I became more invested in following the show each season, it was very clear to me that everyone who went on *MasterChef* shared the same goal: Not only did they love food, but they wanted to change their lives. So on a hope and a prayer, I walked from my tiny south Philly apartment to an open casting call—I gave it my best shot. What followed was a life-altering experience that I wouldn't change for the world.

When Chef Ramsay called my name at the finale, I nearly exploded with emotion. Every day after that, until the finale episode actually aired on television, I would replay the announcement of my win at least ten times before I got out of bed in the morning. That moment was the most important moment of my life so far. It gave me the opportunity to change my life and to take a big step forward toward my goal of being a respected presence in the culinary world.

I was fortunate enough to grow up in an extremely supportive family, but a family that was also full of competitive siblings. My brothers are serious athletes, my sister is an aspiring singer, and I have a background in competitive dance. So when I told my mom I was flying out to LA to take a chance at beginning a serious culinary career, she didn't flinch. She just said, "If you're going to go out there and put your dance career on hold, you have to be the best." With that in mind, I boarded a plane across the country and set out to do exactly what she said.

I was about five years old when I began my love affair with food. My mom let me wear my Snow White costume, and we went to an all-you-can-eat crab buffet. At the time, it was the fanciest I'd ever felt—all dressed up eating this exotic food. From then on, crab legs were my favorite food, and I started to wonder how all of those delicious flavors were created. My earliest memories of actually cooking were with my mom and grandmother. I was the designated "taste tester." As I got older, I began requesting foods that your typical preteen would have little to no interest in, such as calamari, handmade fried ravioli, and sushi. It wasn't until middle school that I began cooking on my own. When I turned sixteen, I made my own birthday cake, which was a really big deal to me at the time. In college I began cooking out of necessity. I threw dorm room dinner parties and asked friends to each bring a dish to share. Eventually, I began arriving at parties with baked goods of some sort, and people were calling me for advice on cooking. Food was a way for me to make friends, start conversations, and gather together with people, just as I had always done with my family.

These recipes are not just a collection of carefully chosen and thought-out dishes—they represent fond memories of my childhood,

Dressed as Snow White at my birthday party. How many five-year-olds do you know who would say crab legs are their favorite food?!

which I have revisited and brought back to life in the pages of this book. From Mom's Smokestacks to Aunt Karen's Chocolate Chip Cookies, I have woven nostalgia into each page and have the highest hopes that you will feel the same comfort that I do as you prepare them.

As an adult, I've taken the warm and loving memories of working at my family's pizza shop and cooking for a group of friends, and I've used the creation of food to add elegance to my everyday life. As you turn these pages, in many of the photos in this book you'll see small pieces of silverware, dishes, and cups that are from my very own kitchen—tokens I've collected that, along with an elevated roasted chicken or some avocado sorbetto, can transform even the smallest dining room table into a bistro in Paris.

Along with my collections of vintage silverware and old-fashioned aprons is my collection of recipes. I have always thought of meals as a way for people to come together, but I've also used as a way to feel fancy while doing something so simple. I hope that this book encourages you to spend time around a table, on a picnic blanket, or at an elegant potluck with the people in your life—be it friends, family, neighbors, or coworkers—and use food as a reason to make every gathering a special memory.

xoxo,

Courtney

THE DISH:
This was the last challenge before the finale. I remember blasting pump-up music that morning to get myself in the zone and ready to compete. It was nerve-wracking, but I was ready to win that MasterChef title.

CHAPTER 1

Breakfast

THE RECIPES

I have books full of diary entries about perfect breakfasts.
Breakfasts complete with lace tablecloths, floral centerpieces, and white china.
Breakfasts outdoors in gardens, and breakfasts indoors during thunderstorms.
To make my diary dreams a reality, I've scoured antique shops for the perfect teaspoons and begged my grandmother to let me have her precious tea sets. I choose
to use sugar cubes because they make my tea taste that much better, and I enjoy
playing vinyl records of old ballets while I savor my breakfast in my south Philly
apartment.

It wasn't always like that, though. Most of my breakfast memories growing up
are shared with my siblings, behind boxes of cereal with cartoons playing in the
background, often finishing our homework just before we left for school.

Whether I am cooking for myself or for someone I care about, it makes me feel
good to know that this first meal is what will set the tone for the rest of the day.
Regardless of what you have in your fridge—or whether or not you have a fancy
tablecloth—don't forget how easy it is to turn bread and water into toast and tea.

Quinoa and Berry Breakfast Cereal

½ cup (100 g) golden quinoa

½ cup (100 g) steel-cut oats

½ cup (100 g) millet

1 tablespoon olive oil

1 tablespoon minced fresh ginger

Zest and juice of 1 lemon

Pinch of salt

1 cup (135 g) hazelnuts

¼ cup (60 ml) pure maple syrup (or honey if you don't have the real deal)

½ cup (120 ml) plain Greek yogurt

¼ teaspoon ground cinnamon

¼ teaspoon freshly grated nutmeg

1 cup (140 g) raspberries

1 cup (140 g) blackberries

When I was studying dance at The University of the Arts and had to make it to my 8:30 a.m. ballet class, I would simply down a shot of espresso, grab my pointe shoes, and jeté out the door. It took some time to realize that I was going to need a little more than caffeine to be able to do all the jumps and turns my teachers were demanding of me, so I came up with this recipe because it has everything required to get me through the morning.

This breakfast is perfect to make the night before, and it keeps in the fridge for about a week, giving you both added energy and extra snooze time. It makes a great on-the-go breakfast, too; when I was in school, I would throw some in a Mason jar and eat it on my walk to class. Feel free to swap out the berries for other fruit, according to the season.

=== SERVES 6 ===

Put the quinoa, oats, and millet in a fine-mesh strainer and run under cool water for about 1 minute.

Heat the oil in a large saucepan over medium-high heat. Add the grains and toast them, stirring frequently, until they begin to smell nutty, 3 to 4 minutes (any longer and they may burn). Add 3 cups (720 ml) water, the ginger, lemon zest, and salt. Bring to a boil, then reduce the heat to low, cover, and simmer for 20 minutes, or until the water is completely absorbed. Remove from the heat and fluff with a fork.

Line a baking sheet with parchment paper and spread the grains on the sheet to cool.

Recipe continues

As the grains are cooling, place the hazelnuts in a skillet over medium-high heat and toast, stirring often, for 3 to 4 minutes, removing the pan from the heat just as you begin to smell their oils releasing (any longer and they may burn). If you like, you may remove the skins by rubbing the hot hazelnuts in a clean kitchen towel (it's okay if some skins are stubborn); otherwise, transfer the nuts to a paper towel–lined plate and let cool.

Spoon the cooled grains into a large bowl. In a medium bowl, whisk together the lemon juice, maple syrup, yogurt, cinnamon, and nutmeg. Pour the yogurt mixture over the cooled grains and toss to coat. Gently fold in the hazelnuts and berries and let the cereal rest for about 30 minutes for the flavors to mingle, or, even better, cover and refrigerate overnight and enjoy it the next day. Alternatively, layer the ingredients as in the photo on page 19.

Oatmeal Risotto

This simple and sweet dish is something I imagine the characters of *A Little Princess* or *The Secret Garden* would eat. It brings with it so much elegance and whimsy, and it really transports you to a different time and place.

This recipe uses Genmaicha tea, nicknamed "popcorn tea," which is a combination of green tea and puffed rice. It's used here in place of the stock that traditional risotto is made with; its flavor enhances the nuttiness of the oats while lending a very light floral fragrance. You can try the same technique using other favorite teas.

1 cup (175 g) steel-cut oats

1 heaping tablespoon genmaicha tea

1 cup (240 ml) milk

1 tablespoon unsalted butter

2 tablespoons brown sugar, plus extra for sprinkling

Chopped walnuts or other nuts and dried mango slices or other dried fruit, for topping

=== SERVES 4 ===

Rinse the oats in a fine-mesh sieve under cold running water.

In a medium saucepan, bring 3 cups (720 ml) water to just under a boil. Place the tea inside a tea infuser. Steep the tea in the water for 4 minutes, then remove the infuser. Keep the tea at a bare simmer.

In a medium saucepan, toast the oats over medium-low heat until they begin to smell nutty, about 2 minutes (any longer and they may burn). Add the tea, ¼ cup (60 ml) at a time, stirring constantly and adding the next ¼ cup (60 ml) after the previous addition has been absorbed completely. Continue until you have used all of the tea and the grains have started to become creamy, 20 to 25 minutes.

After you've made the final addition of tea, immediately add the milk to the pan you made the tea in and heat to just under a simmer; keep over low heat. Begin adding the milk the same way you added the tea, ¼ cup (60 ml) at a time, until you've used all of the milk and the oatmeal is creamy but still al dente, just like risotto, about 15 minutes. Turn off the heat, cover the pan, and let sit for 5 minutes. Remove the lid, add the butter and brown sugar, and stir to incorporate. Spoon into bowls and sprinkle with additional brown sugar and some chopped nuts and dried fruit slices.

Breakfast Tiramisu

1 tablespoon honey

1½ cups (360 ml) plain Greek yogurt

8 ladyfingers

¼ cup (60 ml) brewed espresso or strong coffee, chilled

2 teaspoons cacao nibs

Who wouldn't love to have dessert for breakfast? I would eat it every day if I could. If you think about it, with just a couple of changes—replacing the mascarpone with high-protein Greek yogurt and switching cacao nibs for the cocoa—tiramisu becomes a perfectly acceptable breakfast food. And if you want to balance it out a bit more, you can always add a piece of fruit to complete your plate. This simple-to-make no-cook dish might become your new breakfast favorite.

=================== SERVES 2 ===================

In a small bowl, whisk the honey into the yogurt. Divide the ladyfingers between two shallow bowls, arranging them with the long edges at the bottom of the bowls and leaning one against the next (they should fit snugly), and pour the espresso over the top. Spoon the yogurt over the top of the ladyfingers and garnish with the cacao nibs.

I've always loved dessert—especially for breakfast!

Rice Pancakes

Growing up in our house, there was only one day in the whole year when we were allowed to have pop for breakfast, and that day was Easter. After we searched the house for our Easter baskets and eggs, Mom would open a two-liter bottle of Coca-Cola and my brothers and I would go wild.

Easter was also the only day that Mom cooked us rice pancakes; made from leftover white rice, topped with maple syrup, and served with crispy bacon, this was the Easter breakfast tradition. Looking back, perhaps the idea behind Mom's Easter Sunday Special was that we would crash from our sugar high just in time for church and be able to sit still through the service—which is actually a pretty good reason. When I have my own kids, I plan to continue the tradition.

2 large eggs

¼ cup (60 ml) milk

½ teaspoon salt

4 cups (750 g) cooked white rice

Pure maple syrup, for drizzling

Crispy bacon, for serving

SERVES 4 (makes 8 pancakes)

In a medium bowl, whisk the eggs, milk, and salt. Add the rice and stir with a wooden spoon until evenly coated.

Heat a large nonstick skillet over medium-high heat. Drop the rice mixture by the heaping ¼ cup (60 ml) into the pan, using a spoon to flatten out the rice and give it a shape (you don't want a mountain of rice, but rather a flat disk). Cook until the rice is browned and the pancake is set, about 2 minutes. Flip and cook on the second side for another 2 minutes, or until the rice is browned and slightly crunchy. Transfer to a plate and continue to make pancakes with the remaining rice mixture. (To keep your pancakes warm until serving time, transfer them to a parchment-lined baking sheet placed in a preheated 200°F/95°C oven until ready to serve.) Place on plates and serve drizzled with maple syrup, with strips of bacon alongside.

Strawberry and Rose Scones

Something about scones makes me feel very poetic. White table-cloths, fine china, polished silver, flower vases, and scones: They're the centerpiece of every high tea, a companion to a good book, and just, well, delicious! I love adding rose petals for their incredible fragrance and their ability to perfectly balance out the sweetness of the strawberries. You can find dried rose petals at spice shops and tea shops, and rosewater is readily available at grocery stores. Serve with crème fraîche or sweet butter.

————————————— MAKES 8 —————————————

Preheat the oven to 375°F (175°C) and line a baking sheet with parchment paper.

In a medium bowl, combine the flour, baking powder, and salt. Place the granulated sugar and rose petals in a food processor and pulse until the petals are finely ground into the sugar. Add the rose sugar to the flour mixture and whisk together. Add the butter to the dry mixture and blend with either a pastry blender or your fingertips until the mixture resembles coarse sand. Add the strawberries and mix briefly, taking care not to break down the strawberries. In a small bowl, combine the heavy cream and rose flower water. Pour the cream into the mixture and gently combine with a wooden spoon, being careful not to overmix.

Lightly flour a work surface. Form the scone dough into an 8-inch (20-cm) round and cut the round into 8 triangles. Place the scones on the parchment, a few inches apart. Lightly brush the tops with the beaten egg and sprinkle with the turbinado sugar. Bake for 20 to 25 minutes, until the scones are lightly golden and the centers spring back when touched. Remove the scones from the oven and let cool for 5 minutes. Serve warm or at room temperature. To store the scones, wrap them well in plastic wrap and keep them in the refrigerator for up to 1 week or in the freezer for up to 1 month.

2½ cups (320 g) all-purpose flour

1 tablespoon baking powder

½ teaspoon salt

¼ cup (50 g) granulated sugar

1 heaping tablespoon dried rose petals

6 tablespoons (85 g) unsalted butter, chilled and cut into ½-inch (1.25-cm) cubes

1 cup (160 g) strawberries, hulled and sliced medium thin

1 cup (240 ml) heavy cream

2 teaspoons rose flower water

1 large egg, beaten

1 tablespoon turbinado or crystal sugar

Madeleines pour Madame

For the madeleines

¼ cup (½ stick/55 g) unsalted butter

1 tablespoon dried lavender flowers

2 large eggs

¾ teaspoon vanilla extract

⅛ teaspoon salt

⅓ cup (65 g) sugar

½ cup (60 g) all-purpose flour

For the lemon curd

5 large egg yolks

1 cup (200 g) sugar

Zest of 4 lemons

¾ cup (180 ml) fresh lemon juice

½ cup (1 stick/115 g) unsalted butter, chilled and cut into ½-inch (1.25-cm) pieces

My love of French pastries undoubtedly stems from the incredible French teacher I had in the eighth grade. We called her Madame, and she called us her *petits choux* ("little cabbages"). One day in class Madame was teaching us how to order a meal at a restaurant. She came up to each of us and asked, "*Voudriez-vous une tranche de gâteau?*" ("Would you like a piece of cake?") while holding a madeleine in her hand. I had done my homework the night before, and I replied, "*Oui, Madame, je voudrais une tranche de gâteau, s'il vous plaît!*" and was awarded my first madeleine. Eating it made me feel like a young French girl in Paris—a feeling I'll never forget.

Served with tangy lemon curd, these teeny cakes are the perfect accompaniment for your morning cup of coffee. It's important to note that the recipe asks you to rest the batter; this allows the madeleines to develop their signature "hump" while baking. If you're in a bit of a hurry, you may skip this step; your madeleines will taste equally delicious, but they will come out quite flat on one side.

In memory of Madame, these madeleines are infused with lavender to celebrate her love of the lavender fields in Provence. *Je t'aime, Madame!*

===== MAKES 12 =====

To make the madeleines:

In a small saucepan, melt the butter over low heat. Add the lavender and let steep for 15 minutes. Pour the infused butter through a strainer into a small bowl, pressing a spoon against the lavender flowers to release their floral essence into the butter, and set aside to cool.

In a mixer fitted with the whisk attachment, whisk the eggs, vanilla, and salt until frothy. Gradually add the sugar and continue to whisk until the mixture is thick and pale, 5 to 10 minutes. Sift the flour over the batter and stir it in, being careful not to overmix. Pour the cooled butter into the batter and gently fold to incorporate. Cover the batter with plastic wrap and refrigerate for at least 3 hours or up to 2 days (allowing the madeleines to develop their characteristic hump).

When you are ready to bake the madeleines, preheat the oven to 375F° (200°C) and spray a madeleine pan with cooking spray.

Spoon or pipe the batter into the madeleine pan and bake for 10 to 12 minutes, until the cakes are lightly golden around the edges and the centers spring back when touched. Immediately unmold the madeleines by firmly tapping the pan against the counter. Place the cakes on a cooling rack and allow them to cool to room temperature.

While the madeleine batter is resting, make the lemon curd:
Fill a medium saucepan halfway with water and bring to a boil; this will be your double boiler.

In a medium heatproof bowl, combine the egg yolks and sugar and whisk until smooth, about 1 minute. Add the lemon zest and juice and mix until incorporated.

Place the bowl over the double boiler and gently whisk until the mixture has thickened and coats the back of a spoon, 8 to 10 minutes. Remove the mixture from the heat immediately (or else you'll have scrambled eggs) and stir in the butter one piece at a time, allowing each piece to melt completely before adding the next.

Pour the lemon curd into a container and cover with plastic wrap directly touching the surface of the curd. Refrigerate the lemon curd to set until firm, about 3 hours. Enjoy with the madeleines as you would jam.

Homemade Salted Peanut Butter

3 cups (500 g) raw unsalted shelled and skinned peanuts

¾ teaspoon sea salt, or to taste

2 tablespoons honey

Whenever I ask my brother and the friends he runs with what their favorite food is, they always tell me peanut butter. It's their breakfast, lunch, dinner, and midnight snack. But most important, it's their primary source of energy first thing in the morning to get them through a run.

One of my younger brothers, Colby, is an avid cross-country runner. Where food is my passion, running is his, and he's just as competitive as I am, winning marathons and earning scholarships to universities. Growing up, it was always me cheering for my brothers at sporting events; I never imagined one day I would hear them doing the same for me. Their words of encouragement at the *MasterChef* Finale made me feel like I could do anything.

I like to think this peanut butter will help Colby win many marathons to come. If you want to eat it like Colby would, grab a spoon and dig in. If you want to be daring, try it the way my mom likes it, on toast with crunchy iceberg lettuce. Or, if you want to dress it up, spread it on an English muffin with your favorite jam.

MAKES ABOUT 2 CUPS (400 g)

Preheat the oven to 350°F (175°C) and line a baking sheet with parchment paper.

Spread the peanuts in an even layer over the prepared baking sheet and roast for about 10 minutes, shaking the pan once halfway through, until you begin to smell and see the oils releasing from the peanuts and the peanuts start to turn lightly golden. Remove from the oven promptly (or you risk burning them). Transfer to a plate to cool slightly.

Place all the peanuts in a food processor for smooth peanut butter; for chunky peanut butter, reserve a handful of peanuts to pulse in later. Process for about 5 minutes, stopping to scrape down the sides after each minute or so, until glossy and soft. As the peanuts transform into peanut butter, they will begin to break down, first looking crumbly and dry at the bottom of the machine; then, as the oils release, the almost-peanut-butter will start to stick to the walls of the machine; then the whole mixture will gather into a large ball. Shortly after, as the oils continue to release, the ball will loosen into a fairly smooth puree.

At this point, add the salt and honey and process again for another 3 to 5 minutes, scraping the sides once or twice as needed, to your desired consistency. If you're making chunky peanut butter, add the reserved peanuts and pulse a few times to your desired chunkiness without pureeing them.

Transfer the peanut butter to a jar, cover, and store in the refrigerator for up to 1 month.

THE DISH:
Standing in the *MasterChef* kitchen for the first time as a contestant was so exhilarating! Being in front of the judges made me so nervous that I began standing in ballet poses to stay poised, grounded, and confident. That "crossed ankle" pose you always saw me in is called Third Position.

Crème Brûlée–Stuffed French Toast

3 large eggs

¾ cup (180 ml) heavy cream

1 teaspoon pure vanilla extract

Large pinch of salt

¼ teaspoon ground cinnamon

⅛ teaspoon freshly grated nutmeg

⅓ cup (70 g) mascarpone cheese

6 ounces (170 g) fresh raspberries

4 teaspoons sugar

10 fresh mint leaves, cut into chiffonade

6 (1-inch-/2.5-cm-thick) slices brioche or challah bread, cut into large rounds

Crème brûlée is easily the most well-known French dessert. Rich vanilla custard crowned with a layer of burnt sugar, garnished with a fresh raspberry and a sprig of mint, and served with a silver spoon: a combination that spells perfection. This French toast is no different from your favorite dessert; as you dip the bread slices in the cream base and caramelize some sugar for the desired crunch, you'll be shouting, "*Qu'ils mangent de la brioche!*" ("Let them eat cake!") I like to cut the centers of the bread out with a round cookie cutter or the rim of a glass so the finished crème brûlée will look like a layer cake. And don't waste the bread scraps—turn them into croutons, save them for panzanella (page 71), or toss them in with your strata (page 51).

Tip: Since no one likes to whip cream first thing in the morning, I've given you a little trick you can use to whip small amounts of cream: Simply pour the cream into a Mason jar or any other container with a tight-fitting lid and shake it! If you have little ones in your kitchen, this is a great way to have them participate. Once you're done with breakfast, leftover whipped cream can be saved directly in the container.

===== SERVES 2 =====

Preheat the oven to 200°F (95°C). Line a baking sheet with parchment paper and place it in the oven.

In a large bowl, whisk the eggs with ¼ cup (60 ml) of the heavy cream, the vanilla, and salt. Pour the mixture into a pie plate or baking pan. In a separate bowl, whisk the cinnamon and nutmeg into the mascarpone cheese. In a third bowl, combine all but 6 of the raspberries with 2 teaspoons of the sugar and the mint and set aside to macerate, mashing the berries with a fork a couple of times, as you proceed with the recipe.

Recipe continues

Pour the remaining ½ cup (120 ml) heavy cream into a Mason jar or other jar with a tight-fitting lid and shake until you can't feel the cream moving around anymore, 1 to 2 minutes. Now you're holding a jar of whipped cream—cool, huh?

Heat a large nonstick skillet over medium heat. Two or three at a time, soak both sides of the bread rounds in the egg mixture for 30 seconds each. Place the rounds on the skillet and cook for about 2 minutes, until golden brown, then flip and cook until golden brown on the second side, another minute or so. Place on the prepared baking sheet in the oven to keep warm while you cook the remaining bread slices.

When you've finished cooking both sides of the last two slices, raise the heat to high. Sprinkle 1 teaspoon of the remaining sugar directly onto the hot pan, in about the same size and shape as the toast, and place one slice of toast directly on top of the sugar. Cook for about 10 seconds, until the sugar is caramelized and slightly burnt. Remove from the pan using a slotted spatula and place on a plate, brûléed side up; repeat with the remaining 1 teaspoon sugar and a second toast slice; as the slices cool slightly, that signature crème brûlée "crack" will appear. Leave these two slices to crown your French toast tower.

To serve, place 1 slice of toast on a serving plate and top with one-quarter of the mascarpone cheese and one-quarter of the macerated raspberries. Add another slice, followed by another layer of mascarpone and raspberries. Finish with a brûléed slice and garnish with whipped cream and 3 of the reserved whole raspberries. Repeat with the remaining ingredients to make a second serving.

The Ultimate Sticky Buns

The smell of freshly baked sticky buns takes me directly to Christmas morning. There was something so luxurious about waking to the knowledge that both beautifully wrapped presents and these decadent treats were waiting for me downstairs. Mom would make them the night before and pop them in the oven after we emptied our stockings; by the time we finished opening our presents, they were warm. I would always eat the gooey, nutty side and leave the actual pastry for my dad to dip in his coffee. No one should have to wait until Christmas to enjoy this delicious treat, which is why I'm sharing it with you here.

===== MAKES TWO 10-PIECE RINGS =====

To make the dough:

In a small saucepan, bring the milk to the scalding point and remove it from heat. Add ¼ cup (60 ml) the water and cool to 110°F to 115°F (43°C to 46°C); if it is too hot, it will kill the yeast. Pour the cooled water and milk into the bowl of a stand mixer fitted with the paddle attachment. Add the granulated sugar, sprinkle in the yeast, and whisk together. Dust a few tablespoons of the flour lightly over the top and let stand until the yeast blooms and cracks form across the surface of the flour, about 10 minutes.

Add the remaining flour and the salt to the yeast mixture and blend at medium speed, scraping down the sides of the bowl occasionally, until the batter turns shaggy. Add the eggs one at a time, adding each immediately after the previous one is incorporated. Continue beating the dough at medium speed for about 2 minutes, then add the butter 1 tablespoon at a time, allowing the butter to fully incorporate before adding the next tablespoon; this will take about 5 minutes. Scrape down the sides and bottom of the bowl a few times as you're adding the butter.

Recipe continues

For the dough

¼ cup (60 ml) whole milk

3 tablespoons granulated sugar

1 tablespoon active dry yeast

2¾ cups (350 g) all-purpose flour

1½ teaspoons salt

3 large eggs, at room temperature

12 tablespoons (1½ sticks/ 170 g) unsalted butter, at room temperature

For the filling

1 cup (240 ml) sour cream

1½ teaspoons ground cinnamon

1 cup (220 g) brown sugar

1 cup (115 g) pecans, finely chopped

1 large egg, beaten

For the caramel topping

½ cup (120 ml) honey

½ cup (110 g) brown sugar

4 tablespoons (55 g) unsalted butter

2½ cups (285 g) whole pecans

One of my earliest "cooking" experiences was decorating my own gingerbread house.

Remove the paddle attachment and replace it with the dough hook. Increase the speed to high and beat the dough until you can hear it slapping the sides of the bowl, about 10 minutes. The dough is ready when you can pull a strand into a 2-inch (5-cm) square that forms a translucent "windowpane" of dough that you can see through. For a demonstration, see the how-to photographs for Brioche (page 63).

Spray the inside of a large bowl with cooking spray and scrape the dough into the bowl. Cover with plastic wrap and let rise in a warm, draft-free place until nearly doubled in volume, 1 to 2 hours. When the dough is ready, turn it out onto a lightly floured work surface and press it down into a flat rectangle about 12 by 5 inches (30 by 13 cm). Brush off any excess flour and fold the dough in thirds, as if folding a business letter. Repeat this folding step twice more, then return the dough to the bowl, cover it with plastic wrap, and chill the dough in the refrigerator for 6 hours or overnight before preparing to bake.

To fill the dough:
Remove the dough from the refrigerator and discard the plastic wrap. On a lightly floured work surface, with lightly floured hands, press and roll the dough into a 20-by-16-inch (50-by-40-cm) rectangle, keeping the long side parallel to the edge of the work surface. Brush off any excess flour. Using a flat metal spatula, spread the sour cream over the dough, leaving a 1-inch (2.5-cm) border along

the bottom edge. Sprinkle the cinnamon, brown sugar, and chopped pecans on top of the sour cream. Brush the beaten egg along the bottom edge of the dough. Starting at the top edge, tuck the dough over and begin rolling it toward yourself, tucking and gently rolling back and forth as you go to keep the log nice and tight, sealing it at the egg-brushed bottom edge. Position the log seam side down and set aside while you make the caramel topping.

To make the caramel topping:

Spray two 8-inch (20-cm) round pans with cooking spray.

In a small saucepan, combine the honey, brown sugar, and butter and heat over medium heat until the mixture is melted and fully bubbling, then pour the caramel into the two pans, dividing it equally. Evenly sprinkle the whole pecans over the caramel.

To assemble:

Measure the length of the pecan roll and slice it in half. Slice each half into 10 even pieces and place them in the pans over the caramel, leaving space between the rolls. You should be able to fit 8 pieces around the inside edge of the pan and 2 in the center. Cover the pans loosely with plastic wrap and place them in a warm place to rise for 1½ to 2 hours, until they are doubled in size and poofy to the touch.

To bake the buns:

Preheat the oven to 350°F (175°F).

Place the buns in the oven and bake for 30 minutes, or until golden brown and hollow sounding when tapped. Remove the buns from the oven, place on a cooling rack, and allow to rest for 1 minute. Then immediately invert the pans so the caramel doesn't cool and stick to the bottom of the pan. To serve, break off the sticky buns one at a time. Serve hot out of the oven, at room temperature, or anywhere in between, with coffee or tea for dunking.

Bourbon White Peach Crepes with Thai Basil and Quark

A few years ago, I crossed "go to Paris" off my bucket list. I stayed in a very small hotel in Montparnasse that was next door to a creperie. Every day I had a different kind of crepe, and each came folded up in a little triangle for traveling purposes. Inspired by my trip to Paris, I came back home with the intention of continuing my morning crepe routine, but using new seasonal and local ingredients. This one was my favorite.

This recipe calls for quark, a creamed cheese made from whole milk rather than cream. You can impart any flavor you like to it by adding herbs, honey, or spices, and it is also delicious when spread on bagels and toast. You can find quark in specialty food stores, farmers' markets, and food co-ops. If it is unavailable, you may substitute mascarpone, ricotta, or soft goat cheese. Fresh Thai basil flowers may be a little tricky to find; you'll have your best luck at a farmers' market or Asian market. If you choose to substitute Italian basil for the Thai basil, you will only need to use half as much, as Italian basil is very powerful and can overwhelm the dish.

=========== SERVES 4 ===========

To make the crepe batter:
In a medium bowl, whisk the eggs, milk, ½ cup (120 ml) water, and the salt. Gradually add the flour and whisk until there are no lumps remaining. Pour the melted butter in a circle around the edges of the batter and fold it in with a rubber spatula. Set the batter aside to rest while you prepare the filling, or refrigerate in an airtight container for up to 1 day; whisk before using (if you're preparing the batter ahead of time, add the butter just before making the crepes).

Recipe continues

For the crepes

2 large eggs

½ cup (120 ml) whole milk

¼ teaspoon salt

1 cup (125 g) all-purpose flour

3 tablespoons unsalted butter, melted and cooled

For the filling

4 large ripe white peaches

¼ cup (50 g) sugar

1 tablespoon unsalted butter

2 tablespoons bourbon

Large pinch of salt

For serving

1 cup (8 ounces/227 g) quark

6 fresh Thai basil leaves, or 3 regular basil leaves, cut into chiffonade

4 teaspoons honey

8 Thai basil flowers, or 3 regular basil leaves, cut into chiffonade (optional)

Cut the peaches in half as you would an avocado and remove the pits. Cut each half into 4 wedges. Using a very sharp knife, remove the skin from all but one of the peaches (peeling is recommended to avoid pieces of chewy peach skin, which may or may not be your desired texture): Hold a peach wedge skin side down and slide the knife between the skin and flesh, staying as close to the skin as possible and flattening out the peach wedge as you go to release the skin. (If your peaches are very ripe, you might be able to peel them with your fingers.) Repeat with the remaining wedges and then chop them. Thinly slice the unpeeled peach and set aside for garnish.

Heat a large skillet over medium-high heat. Add the chopped peaches and sprinkle with the sugar. Cook for about 10 minutes, using a fork to gently mash the peaches and adding the butter as the peaches break down. When the peaches take on a texture resembling chutney, add the bourbon and salt and cook until the bourbon is absorbed into the peaches, about 3 minutes. Remove the pan from the heat and set aside while you cook the crepes.

Heat a 9-inch (23-cm) crepe pan or nonstick or well-seasoned cast-iron skillet over medium heat. Drop about 3 tablespoons of the crepe batter into the pan, and with the flat bottom of a glass or stainless-steel measuring cup, spread the batter into a thin circle 6 to 7 inches (15 to 18 cm) in diameter (don't worry if the crepes aren't perfectly circular; oblong and irregular shapes are fine, too).

Cook the crepe for about 2 minutes, until the top appears set and the bottom is firm. Using a rubber spatula, loosen the edges of the crepe, flip it, and cook for about 45 seconds, until the bottom is firm and golden brown in spots, then transfer the crepe to a plate. Repeat with the remaining batter, adding the crepes to the plate as you finish them, to make 8 crepes.

To make the toppings and serve:
In a small bowl, combine the quark and basil. Drop a spoonful of the quark onto the center of a plate. Place a crepe on a cutting board and fill it by adding a stripe of the white peach filling across the edge of the crepe closest to you and rolling away from you. Place the crepe seam side down on a cutting board and cut it in half at an angle. Repeat with a second crepe. Assemble the crepe halves, seam sides down, on top of the quark and top with 2 of the reserved peach slices. Drizzle with 1 teaspoon of the honey and garnish with a few scattered basil flowers, if you wish. Repeat with the remaining ingredients to make 4 servings.

Cinnamon Toast and Perfect Scrambled Eggs

1 tablespoon sugar

½ teaspoon ground cinnamon

3 tablespoons unsalted butter

2 large eggs

2 slices white bread

¼ teaspoon salt, or to taste

1 teaspoon finely chopped fresh chives

Mom used to keep a small bowl of cinnamon and sugar next to our toaster oven. We would sprinkle it on slices of buttered toast, which we ate with scrambled eggs that we cooked in the microwave. This simple breakfast was something we could make on our own, even in elementary school, and then teach our younger siblings when they entered kindergarten. My youngest brother, Cooper, just turned seven, and he's learned to make this breakfast, except, as a little MasterChef in training, he demands that we pretend to be judges and critique his creation.

Instead of cooking your eggs in a microwave like we used to, I'm going to show you a technique for making what I consider to be perfect scrambled eggs. The trick is not scrambling the eggs before you put them in the pan and adding a good chunk of butter. With my kitchen filled with the aromatic scents, I eat this simple and delicious breakfast now with a cup of warm tea and treat myself to the morning paper and a vase full of freshly cut flowers.

SERVES 1

In a small bowl, combine the sugar and cinnamon. Set aside.

Heat a small skillet over medium heat and add 2 tablespoons of the butter. Crack the eggs into a medium bowl, and just before the butter is completely melted, add the eggs to the skillet. Using a rubber spatula, stir the eggs, breaking the yolks and incorporating the melted butter.

Meanwhile, pop the bread in the toaster.

Keep stirring the eggs until they're velvety and creamy, about 3 minutes; do not overcook them or you'll wind up with a chopped-up omelet instead of scrambled eggs. Season with the salt.

Butter the toast with the remaining 1 tablespoon butter and sprinkle the cinnamon sugar on top. Place on a plate; serve the eggs alongside and garnish with the chives.

Eggs Benedict

Eggs Benedict—poached eggs atop Canadian bacon and English muffins, smothered in hollandaise—is the quintessential fancy brunch dish. But who wants to go through the trouble of poaching eggs and nearly breaking a sweat putting together the sometimes-finicky hollandaise before breakfast? You do! Though it does take some time, with a little practice and a few cups of coffee beforehand, making eggs Benedict isn't all that difficult, so fear not!

Yes, hollandaise requires attention, but that doesn't mean it's hard to make—it just means you can't walk away from the stove for ten minutes. Whisk your eggs vigorously over barely simmering water to thicken them, then slowly add the butter in a thin stream to emulsify the sauce to perfection. Once the hollandaise is created, you can use the same pot of simmering water to poach your eggs; you'll save on cleanup, and the hollandaise will keep while you complete the recipe.

And as for that poaching vortex that seems so terrifying? Just give the water a good stir to gain momentum. You'll notice that I don't whip my poaching liquid; I just stir it with enough force for the whites to envelop the yolks, and that's all you need.

=== SERVES 2 ===

To poach the eggs:

Add the vinegar to the water in the pan you cooked the hollandaise in and bring to a bare simmer (most poached egg recipes call for a wide saucepan, but I find that the eggs cook just as easily in a smaller pan). Use a slotted spoon to quickly stir the water clockwise three times. This will create a vortex, which will ensure that your egg is poached properly. Crack an egg as close to the water as possible so it doesn't splash (or crack each egg into an individual small bowl or teacup) and gently tip it into the vortex (see photo 1 on page 42). The egg will swirl around the pan a few times and then come together in the center of the pan; poach the egg for about 2 minutes, until the white is set and the yolk is cooked to your liking. Remove the egg with

Recipe continues

For the eggs

1 tablespoon apple cider vinegar

4 large eggs

For the hollandaise

3 large egg yolks

½ cup (1 stick/115 g) unsalted butter, melted

2 to 3 teaspoons fresh lemon juice

¼ to ½ teaspoon hot sauce, to taste

¼ teaspoon salt, or to taste

For the bacon and English muffins

1 tablespoon plus 4 teaspoons unsalted butter

4 slices Canadian bacon

2 English muffins, split and toasted

Salt

Cayenne pepper (optional)

the slotted spoon (see photo 2 on page 42) and transfer to a paper towel–lined plate to rest while you poach the remaining eggs and cook the bacon. If any stray egg white remains after you poach an egg, scoop it out with the slotted spoon before adding the next egg.

To make the hollandaise:

Find a small saucepan and a nonreactive bowl that is slightly larger than the saucepan. Add enough water to the pan so you can also poach the eggs, but not so much that it will touch the bottom of the bowl, and bring to a simmer; immediately reduce the heat to low and keep at a bare simmer. While the water is heating up, add the egg yolks to the bowl and whisk until they are thickened but still a little liquidy, about 2 minutes (see photo 3 on page 42). Place the bowl over the simmering water, making sure the bottom of the bowl doesn't come in contact with the water, and whisk vigorously until the eggs are thickened to a creamy salad-dressing consistency, 2 to 4 minutes. Remove the bowl from over the water and keep whisking to slightly cool the eggs, then gently add the melted butter—just a trickle at first (it will look oily in the beginning, but it will all be incorporated at the end), then in a thin, slow stream (see photo 4 on page 42), whisking vigorously all the time, until emulsified. Whisk in the lemon juice, hot sauce, and salt; taste and adjust the seasonings if needed. If the hollandaise comes out too thick, more like mayonnaise, return it to the heat for a few seconds and whisk to restore its saucelike consistency.

To cook the bacon and assemble:

In a large skillet, melt 1 tablespoon of the butter over medium heat. Add the bacon and cook until crisp, about 2 minutes on each side; transfer to a plate. While the bacon is cooking, toast the English muffins and spread each half with 1 teaspoon butter. Place a slice of bacon on each muffin half, place an egg over each bacon slice (see photo 4 on page 42), sprinkle with salt, and spoon the hollandaise on top. For an extra pop of color, sprinkle a touch of cayenne on top of the hollandaise.

Pour any remaining hollandaise into a pitcher or small bowl and serve it at the table for diners to drizzle over their eggs as they like. Any remaining hollandaise will keep, covered and refrigerated, for up to 1 day; reheat by whisking over a double boiler in the same manner you prepared the hollandaise.

Creamed Kale and Eggs

1 medium leek

2 tablespoons unsalted butter

3 cups (40 g) roughly chopped kale leaves, all stems removed

¾ cup (180 ml) heavy cream

¼ cup (30 g) grated Parmesan cheese

4 large eggs

Salt and freshly ground black pepper

This recipe, featuring hearty kale and beautiful leeks topped with fresh eggs, is one of my favorites. It's so easy and delicious that after you've made it once, you'll likely be turning to it again and again. I like to cook mine in a cast-iron skillet, starting on the stovetop and finishing the dish in the oven. This not only cooks the eggs perfectly but makes for a great presentation, too (just warn everyone that the pan is hot!).

SERVES 2

Preheat the oven to 400°F (200°F).

Cut off the root end and the dark green leaves from the leek. Slice the leek in half lengthwise, then slice it crosswise into pieces ¼ inch (6 mm) thick.

Heat a medium ovenproof skillet, preferably cast-iron, over medium heat, add the butter, and swirl to melt it. Add the leeks and cook, stirring often, until they caramelize, 5 to 7 minutes. Add the kale, increase the heat to medium-high, and cook until the kale is wilted, 1 to 2 minutes. Add the cream and cheese and toss to coat. Crack the eggs evenly into the pan, season with salt and pepper, and transfer the pan to the oven. Bake until the egg whites are firm but the yolks are still soft, about 7 minutes. Remove from the oven and serve straight out of the pan, with some toast for soaking up all the delicious juices.

Prosciutto-Wrapped Asparagus with Poached Eggs, Potatoes, and Chamomile Butter

This is a breakfast I sometimes make as a special treat for myself. Although it's extremely simple to put together, the chamomile butter is what makes this dish top-tier. Be sure to purchase chamomile tea that contains only the leaves so that when you incorporate it into the butter, there are no chewy or sharp stems.

Don't be afraid to use your hands to eat the asparagus spears—asparagus is traditionally a finger food—and the contrast of the salty prosciutto and the honey will have you happily licking your fingers. You'll be surprised how easy it is to make the chamomile butter, and once you taste it, you'll find yourself drizzling it on everything from toast to vegetables.

===== SERVES 2 =====

Fill a medium saucepan with water, add the garlic and shallot, and bring to a boil over high heat. Add the potatoes, reduce the heat to medium, and simmer until the potatoes arc fork-tender, about 15 minutes. Drain and discard the garlic and shallot. Set the potatoes aside.

Meanwhile, fill a small saucepan three-quarters full with water (most poached egg recipes call for a wide saucepan, but I find that the eggs cook just as easily in a smaller pan). Add the vinegar and bring to a bare simmer. Use a slotted spoon to quickly stir the water clockwise three times. This will create a vortex, which will ensure that your egg is poached properly. Crack an egg as close to the water as possible so it doesn't splash (or crack each egg into an individual small bowl or teacup) and gently tip it into the vortex (see photo 1 on page 42). The egg will swirl around the pan a few times and then

Recipe continues

2 cloves garlic, smashed and peeled

1 shallot

2 new potatoes

1 tablespoon apple cider vinegar

2 large eggs

8 thin slices prosciutto (4 ounces/115 g)

8 thin asparagus stalks

4 tablespoons (½ stick/55 g) unsalted butter

2 pure chamomile tea bags (with leaves only)

1 teaspoon honey

Pinch of salt

come together in the center of the pan; poach the egg for about 2 minutes, until the white is set and the yolk is cooked to your liking. Remove the egg with the slotted spoon and transfer to a paper towel—lined plate to rest while you poach the second egg. If any stray egg white remains after you poach the first egg, scoop it out with the slotted spoon before adding the second egg.

Lay the prosciutto out flat on a work surface and snap the ends off the asparagus. Starting at the bottom of an asparagus stalk, wrap the prosciutto tightly up the spear at an angle, leaving the tip peeking out at the end. Repeat with the remaining prosciutto and asparagus.

Heat a large skillet over medium-high heat. Add the prosciutto-wrapped asparagus and sear on all sides, about 7 minutes, turning with tongs as the asparagus colors. Make sure you hear the pan sizzle as you rotate the asparagus to ensure a good sear.

While the asparagus is cooking, melt the butter in a small saucepan over medium heat; cut open the tea bags and empty the contents into the melting butter. Add the honey and salt and stir to incorporate. Remove from the heat, pour the butter into a small bowl, and let the tea infuse the liquid (no need to strain). Do not wipe out the pan; reserve it with the remains of the butter to sauté the potatoes.

Cut the potatoes into bite-size pieces. Reheat the pan you melted the butter in over medium heat, add the potatoes, and cook, stirring, for about 5 minutes to get some color on them. Lower the heat and keep warm.

To serve, place half of the potatoes in the center of a plate. Top with 4 prosciutto-wrapped asparagus stalks arranged into a cross shape. Nestle a poached egg on top of the potatoes and asparagus and use a spoon to drizzle chamomile butter over the egg and around the dish. Repeat with the remaining ingredients for the second serving. Save any remaining chamomile butter to spread over toast or use it instead of plain butter the next time you sauté vegetables.

Sausage and Apple Strata

Do you ever play the game of looking in the fridge, then looking in the cupboard, then looking in the fridge again to see if anything has changed? I do it all the time. Strata is a wonderful way to use up leftover crusty bread and other lonely ingredients you have lying around in the kitchen, and when you're all done, you've got a delicious meal and haven't let a thing go to waste. Since it requires overnight resting (this allows the bread to absorb the egg mixture), this is a great dish to make ahead of time and bring to a brunch potluck; just ask the host to have the oven preheated for you when you arrive.

SERVES 8

In a large skillet, heat the oil over medium-high heat. Add the sausage and cook, breaking it apart with a wooden spoon, until browned, about 10 minutes. Using a slotted spoon, transfer to a large bowl.

Reduce the heat to medium and add the apples, onion, and sage to the fat in the pan (add a little oil if your sausage didn't release much fat). Cook, stirring often, until the onions are translucent and the apples are softened, about 10 minutes. Season with salt and pepper. Remove from the pan, add to the browned sausage, and cool completely. Add the bread cubes to the bowl and toss well.

In a separate large bowl, whisk the eggs, milk, and nutmeg until frothy and season with salt and pepper. Pour the mixture over the sausage and bread, tossing to coat the bread pieces well. Transfer the mixture to a 9-by-13-inch (23-by-33-cm) baking dish. Cover with foil and refrigerate for at least 8 hours or overnight.

Preheat the oven to 375°F (190°C). Take the strata out of the refrigerator and give it a good stir.

Place the strata in the oven and bake for 20 minutes. Remove the foil and bake for another 20 minutes, or until the bread is browned. Serve immediately or let cool slightly.

1 tablespoon olive oil, plus extra if needed

4 sweet Italian sausage links, casings removed

2 Granny Smith apples, cored and chopped

1 medium yellow onion, chopped

10 fresh sage leaves, cut into chiffonade

Salt and freshly ground black pepper

½ baguette, torn into about 2-inch (5-cm) cubes

6 large eggs

1 cup (240 ml) milk

¼ teaspoon freshly grated nutmeg

Ham and Cheddar Pastry Squares

1 (9-by-9-inch/23-by-23-cm)
puff pastry sheet, cut into
9 squares

1 large egg

¼ teaspoon salt

4 ounces (115 g) very thinly
sliced ham

1 cup (90 g) shredded cheddar
cheese

These little pastries are perfect to bring along for a morning picnic, or
to pop in your mouth on your way out the door. They're quite simple
to make, and they will surely impress. For this recipe I use packaged
puff pastry, but if you'd like to make your own, go for it! Feel free to
get a little creative and change up the fillings—that's what cooking is
all about!

=========== MAKES 9 PASTRIES ===========

Preheat the oven to 400°F (200°C) and line a baking sheet with
parchment paper. Place the puff pastry squares on the prepared
baking sheet.

In a small bowl, whisk together the egg and salt to make an egg
wash. Using a pastry brush, brush the egg wash over the top ½-inch
(1.25-cm) border of the puff pastry squares. Top each square with
a ham slice, placing it nicely folded in the center to keep a ¼-inch
(6-mm) border. Sprinkle the cheese over the top of the ham on
each pastry.

Place in the oven and bake for 12 to 15 minutes, until the pastry
has puffed and is golden brown. Transfer the pastries to a cooling
rack to set for 5 minutes. Serve warm or at room temperature.
The pastries can be covered and stored in the refrigerator for up
to 2 days and rewarmed before serving.

Really Good Chai

The first time I had chai was with my high school girlfriends in a small Middle Eastern restaurant. We sat on pillows, ate with our hands, and spent the entire meal laughing. At the end of our meal, we were given small mugs of foamy, aromatic chai with an explosion of spices. Cardamom was already a favorite spice of mine, but I was surprised to taste peppercorns in this sweet preparation. This recipe is perfect for a blustery day, curled up in your comfiest clothes and letting the heat from the mug warm your hands while the drink warms your belly.

=== SERVES 2 ===

To make the spice blend:
Combine the spices in a medium saucepan. Place over medium heat for about 2 minutes, until you can smell their fragrant oils being released.

To make the chai:
Pour the milk over the spices, add the tea bags and sugar, and bring just to a gentle boil.

While the milk is heating up, warm two mugs by filling them with hot water and letting them sit until the milk is ready.

As soon as the chai mixture comes to a boil, turn off the heat, pour out the hot water from the mugs, and place a ginger coin in the bottom of each mug. Remove the tea bags from the milk. Place a small tea strainer over one mug and pour half of the infused milk through the strainer. Pour the rest of the milk into the second mug, making sure all of the spices make their way out of the pan and into the strainer. With the spices still in the strainer, rinse them off under cool running water and place on a small paper towel–lined plate to dry completely so you can use them again. The spice blend can be used up to five times, or until you feel that it has lost its strength. Serve the chai garnished with nutmeg.

For the spice blend
1 cinnamon stick

2 whole star anise

½ vanilla bean

10 cardamom pods

6 whole cloves

4 whole black peppercorns

For the chai
3 cups (720 ml) whole milk

2 black tea bags

2 tablespoons sugar

2 thin slices fresh ginger, cut into coins

Freshly grated nutmeg

Fancy Sunday Brunch

Brunch is just about the only thing that can pull me out of bed on a weekend morning. What more of an excuse do I need to dress up, socialize with my girlfriends, and enjoy delicious food? There's something about the attention paid to brunch that makes it feel so special. Whether I choose to use my nicest table linens or pick some fresh flowers for the centerpiece, I always go the extra mile for brunch, and you can, too, with this easy menu that will have your friends asking for seconds!

CHAPTER 2

Lunch

THE RECIPES

In the summertime, lunch is my favorite meal of the day.

I'll pack my great-grandmother's picnic basket—not forgetting a blanket and a good book—and I'll spend the day at Logan Square, where the water fountains are reminiscent of those at Versailles. Often, my friends will join me, and we'll bask in the sunlight all day long, nibbling on our lunch and daydreaming.

You'll notice a lot of the recipes in this chapter are warm-weather related, and that's not by accident. I have so many memories of eating lunch with my family during the summer on Seneca Lake. But these recipes hold up even on the most gray, chilly days, when something like the chickpea salad will let you close your eyes and imagine you're bathed in sunshine.

I have great hopes that you'll bring Mom's Big Green Bowl Macaroni Salad to your family's next picnic, and I also hope that you're inspired enough to order pigs' ears from your butcher to make the dish that opened my finale meal. Lunch doesn't always have to come out of a brown bag—nor does it have to be prepared in a rush. Take the time to carefully prepare these recipes, and you'll see how easily you can make your midday meal an event to remember.

Brioche

¼ cup (60 ml) whole milk

3 tablespoons sugar

1 tablespoon active dry yeast

2¾ cups (350 g) all-purpose flour

1½ teaspoons fine salt

3 large eggs, at room temperature, plus 1 large egg, beaten with 1 teaspoon water (for the egg wash)

12 tablespoons (1½ sticks/ 170 g) unsalted butter, at room temperature

1½ teaspoons Maldon salt

We've all heard the famous quote: "Let them eat cake." But did you know that the political cartoon written about Marie Antoinette wasn't actually referring to cake? Lost in translation, the actual word used was *brioche*. Because brioche is made from a dough rich in butter and eggs, it was more expensive to make than bread. How's that for food for thought?

This recipe makes two loaves, which you can use in recipes throughout the book, such as Fancy BLTs (page 68), Crème Brûlée French Toast (page 30), and Grilled Cheese Toasties (page 66).

= MAKES TWO 8-BY-4-INCH (20-by-10-cm) LOAVES =

In a small saucepan, bring the milk to the scalding point and remove it from the heat. Add ¼ cup (60 ml) water and cool to 110°F to 115°F (43°C to 46°C); if it is too hot, it will kill the yeast. Pour the cooled water and milk into the bowl of a stand mixer fitted with the paddle attachment. Add the sugar, sprinkle in the yeast, and whisk together. Dust a few tablespoons of the flour lightly over the top and let stand until the yeast blooms and cracks form across the surface of the flour, about 10 minutes.

Add the remaining flour and the fine salt to the yeast mixture and beat at medium speed, scraping down the sides of the bowl occasionally, until the batter turns shaggy. Add the 3 eggs one at a time, adding each immediately after the previous one is incorporated. Continue beating the dough at medium speed for about 2 minutes, then add the butter 1 tablespoon at a time, allowing the butter to fully incorporate before adding the next tablespoon; this will take about 5 minutes. Scrape down the sides and bottom of the bowl a few times as you're adding the butter.

Remove the paddle attachment and replace it with the dough hook. Increase the speed to high and beat the dough until you can hear it slapping the sides of the bowl, about 10 minutes. The dough is ready

Recipe continues

when you can pull a strand into a 2-inch (5-cm) rectangle that forms a translucent "windowpane" of dough that you can see through (see photos 1 and 2 on page 63).

Spray the inside of a large bowl with nonstick cooking spray and scrape the dough into the bowl. Cover with plastic wrap and let rise in a warm, draft-free place until nearly doubled in volume, 1 to 2 hours. When the dough is ready, turn it out onto a lightly floured work surface and press the dough down into a flat rectangle about 12 by 5 inches (30 by 13 cm). Brush off any excess flour and fold the dough in thirds, as if folding a business letter. Repeat this folding step twice more, then return the dough to the bowl, cover it with plastic wrap, and chill it in the refrigerator for 6 hours or overnight before preparing to bake. The dough may also be wrapped airtight in plastic wrap and frozen for up to 1 month. Allow the dough to thaw overnight in the refrigerator before using.

Spray two loaf pans with cooking spray and divide the dough into 12 equal-size pieces, rolling them gently into little spheres (see photos 3 and 4 on page 63). Place 6 spheres in each loaf pan in a staggered formation and cover loosely with plastic wrap. Allow the dough to rise once more for 1 to 2 hours, until doubled in volume.

Preheat the oven to 375°F (190°C).

Gently brush the tops of the loaves with the egg wash, being careful not to deflate them. Sprinkle the Maldon salt on top.

Bake until the brioche is deep golden brown in color and the internal temperature is 200°F (38°C), about 30 minutes. Let cool; serve barely warm or at room temperature. Brioche is best enjoyed the day it is baked, or stored at room temperature, tightly wrapped in plastic wrap, for 1 or 2 days. It can also be wrapped tightly in plastic and kept frozen for up to 1 month. Thaw the frozen brioche, still wrapped, at room temperature.

Grilled Cheese Toasties

1 tablespoon olive oil

1 cup (100 g) small broccoli
florets (about ½ small head)

Pinch of salt

2 tablespoons unsalted butter,
softened

4 slices Brioche (page 60)
or other bread of your choice

4 slices pepper Jack cheese,
cut to fit the size of your bread

1 ripe avocado, sliced

Potato chips and pickle spears,
for serving (optional)

Every morning before filming *MasterChef*, Yaz, one of the producers, would come in to say good morning and make sure we were ready for the day. And every morning she was eating a grilled cheese sandwich that we all would have died to sink our teeth into . . . so cheesy, so crunchy, so many rich flavors melting together. Since I never had the opportunity to make grilled cheese on *MasterChef*, I'm going to share this one with you . . . and her!

=== SERVES 2 ===

Heat the oil in a large skillet over medium heat. Add the broccoli and salt and sauté until the broccoli is lightly browned and softened but still al dente, about 5 minutes. Transfer to a paper towel–lined plate.

Wipe out the pan and return it to medium heat. Butter one side of each piece of bread and build the sandwiches directly in the pan: Place 2 bread slices in the pan, buttered side down, then layer each with one slice of cheese, half of the avocado, half of the broccoli, and a second slice of cheese. Finish with another bread slice, buttered side up. Toast for about 3 minutes, pressing down on the sandwiches with a spatula to give them a good sear on the bottom, until the bread is browned and the bottom slice of cheese has melted. Carefully flip, so as not to lose any of the filling, and cook until the remaining cheese is melted, about 3 minutes more. Transfer the sandwiches to a cutting board and cut on an angle. If you like, serve with potato chips and a pickle spear.

Pulled Pork Sandwiches

Every summer, my aunt Michele has a summer solstice party. Our entire family gathers at Lake Ontario, which is so large it looks like the ocean. The day is always filled with sunshine, hilarious games, and great food. As the day ends, we all watch the sunset together, and if it's a clear night, we look for that famous green flash on the horizon as the sun sets over the water. It's a tradition we look forward to every year, marking the end of school and the beginning of summer.

I came up with this recipe with the intention of serving it at our next summer solstice party, in the hopes that I can persuade the family to stray from the traditional hamburger and try something a little different that will spice things up. With my new title of MasterChef, I hope they'll happily agree.

═══════════════ SERVES 8 ═══════════════

To make the pulled pork:

In a small bowl, combine the brown sugar, paprika, cayenne, and salt. Place the pork butt on a large plate and rub it all over with the brown sugar–spice mixture. Place the pork in a slow cooker and pour the beer into the bottom of the cooker. Cover and cook on low for 8 to 10 hours, until the meat pulls away easily with a fork. Remove the pork from the cooker, place on a serving dish, and shred with two forks. If you like, add some of the braising liquid for added flavor and juiciness.

To make the barbecue sauce:

Combine the ingredients in a small saucepan over medium-low heat, bring to a simmer, and simmer just until the sugar has melted. Remove from the heat and transfer to a bowl or squeeze bottle.

To assemble the sandwiches:

Top the bottom halves of the buns with a generous amount of pulled pork, spoon or squeeze the barbecue sauce over the meat, and finish the sandwiches with the top bun halves. Serve with potato chips, if you like.

For the pulled pork

3 tablespoons brown sugar

2 teaspoons sweet paprika

1 teaspoon ground cayenne

1 tablespoon salt

1 (5-pound/2.25-kg) pork butt roast

1 (12-ounce/360-ml) bottle beer (any type you like; lagers and stouts are good choices)

For the barbecue sauce

1 cup (240 ml) ketchup

½ cup (110 g) firmly packed brown sugar

1 teaspoon Worcestershire sauce

1 tablespoon apple cider vinegar

Salt and freshly ground black pepper

8 sesame seed buns, split and toasted

Potato chips, for serving (optional)

Fancy BLTs

8 slices pancetta

2 medium heirloom tomatoes, in contrasting colors

Salt and freshly cracked black pepper

½ cup (120 ml) mayonnaise

Zest and juice of 1 lime

8 slices Brioche (page 60) or any sandwich bread you have on hand

1 head baby gem lettuce, leaves separated

When I was in kindergarten, I thought BLT stood for "bread, lettuce, and tomato." It was the easiest lunch to remember how to make. I could do it by myself, and when I got to school I would find the napkin love notes my mom somehow snuck into my lunch box. To make sure the bread wouldn't get soggy from the tomato juices, I made my lunch the same way every time: bread, mayo, lettuce, tomato, lettuce, mayo, bread. Which is why I thought it was so amazing that during the Diner Takeover challenge, Chef Elliot made a comment about how building sandwiches is like architecture.

For this recipe, I've elevated the BLT staples by using pancetta slices, baby gem lettuce, and heirloom tomatoes. Even the mayo gets an upgrade with the addition of lime juice for extra tang. Make one for your special someone's lunch box, and don't forget the napkin love note.

=== SERVES 4 ===

Heat a large skillet over medium-high heat. Working in two batches, add the pancetta and cook until crisp, about 3 minutes. With a slotted spoon, transfer to a paper towel–lined plate to cool.

Slice the tomatoes ¼ inch (6 mm) thick and season lightly with salt and pepper. In a small bowl, mix together the mayonnaise, lime zest and juice, and a sprinkle of salt. Toast the bread gently in a toaster, or in a preheated 350°F (175°C) oven for about 5 minutes, until crisp.

To build the sandwiches, spread the mayonnaise evenly over each toast slice, and layer a lettuce leaf, 2 tomato slices (one of each color), 2 pancetta slices, and another lettuce leaf over 4 of the bread slices. Top with the remaining lime-mayo-smeared toast, cut in half on an angle, and serve.

Panzanella

Panzanella is a rustic Italian salad made from day-old crusty bread that's softened by the juices of fresh tomatoes and tossed with basil and some good balsamic vinegar. I like to add olives, marinated artichokes, roasted red peppers, and cornichons for some added crunch, but feel free to change it up by including other ingredients such as grilled shrimp or hot peppers to turn this traditional dish into something new and unexpected. As long as you start with a base of good bread and juicy fresh tomatoes, your panzanella is destined to be a tasty one. Because it doesn't contain any cheese, this salad can stand up to the summer heat and is excellent for a picnic or barbecue.

Fresh tomatoes, which are the heart and soul of this dish, are my favorite summer food, and I am always searching Philly's farmers' markets for them. The smell of the tomatoes fresh on the vine is the epitome of the season to me.

If you aren't in the habit of eating olives, the Castelvetrano, a beautiful bright green olive that is mild in flavor and meaty in texture, is a great place to start. Castelvetranos should be easy to find in your grocery store's olive bar, but if they are unavailable, any fresh, pitted, and un-stuffed olive will do—just taste one first to make sure you like it!

½ (16-ounce/450-g) loaf Italian bread, torn into pieces

2½ tablespoons olive oil, plus extra for drizzling

Sea salt and freshly ground black pepper

4 ripe tomatoes, preferably on the vine

¼ cup (20 g) Castelvetrano olives, pitted and sliced

2 tablespoons sliced cornichons

1 roasted red bell pepper, thinly sliced lengthwise

6 marinated artichoke heart quarters

1 tablespoon balsamic vinegar

4 fresh basil leaves

===== SERVES 4 =====

Line a baking sheet with parchment paper. If you are planning ahead, set the bread pieces on the sheet in a single layer and leave on the counter overnight to dry (if your bread is particularly crusty or you don't have the time, you can skip this step).

Preheat the oven to 350°F (175°C).

Recipe continues

Place the bread pieces in a large bowl, toss with the oil, and season with salt and black pepper. Spread the pieces out on the baking sheet in a single layer, place in the oven, and bake for about 15 minutes, until they are dried and very lightly browned. Transfer the sheet to a cooling rack while you prepare the rest of the salad.

Chop the tomatoes into bite-size pieces and place them in a large serving bowl; make sure to include all the juices from the tomatoes, as the juices are what's going to soften the bread. Salting the tomatoes will extract their juices, too, creating a nice dressing for your salad, so season generously with salt and black pepper. Add the olives, cornichons, bell pepper, artichoke hearts, and vinegar and toss to combine the ingredients; set aside to marinate for about 10 minutes.

Tear the basil leaves into pieces and add them to the salad. Add the bread and toss to coat. Spoon into bowls, drizzle with oil, and serve immediately.

Arugula and Goat Cheese Salad with Pickled Beets

To quote *Jitterbug Purfume* by Tom Robbins, "The beet is the most intense of vegetables . . . you can't squeeze blood out of a turnip." I was first introduced to beets by my college friend Monica; I had kept them at arm's length and refused to cook them at home because I was afraid of their staining power. But I learned quickly that they aren't as messy as one might think, and they can brighten up so many different dishes.

The pickled beets are delicious on their own, but with the addition of goat cheese, their tang is slightly subdued and the arugula's natural spice makes for a perfect balance. The crunch of the pistachio is a welcome balance to the creaminess of the cheese, making a wonderful blend of flavors and textures. The pickling liquid left at the bottom of the bowl would make a great aioli or a salad dressing—should you feel adventurous, give it a try!

=== SERVES 4 ===

To make the pickled beets:

Place the beets in a large saucepan and add water to cover by a few inches. Bring to a boil over high heat, then lower the heat and simmer for about 1 hour, until a knife inserted in the center of a beet meets with no resistance. Remove the beets from the pan and drain, reserving 1 cup (240 ml) of the cooking water. Cool the beets until cool enough to handle, then peel off the skins using your hands (I recommend wearing gloves if you don't want your fingers stained). Cool completely, then cut into 1-inch (2.5-cm) pieces and place in a large heatproof bowl.
Recipe continues

For the pickled beets
3 medium red beets

1 cup (240 ml) apple cider vinegar

¼ cup (50 g) sugar

3 sprigs fresh thyme

½ teaspoon coriander seeds

½ teaspoon fennel seeds

½ teaspoon mustard seeds

¼ teaspoon ground allspice

For the salad
2 tablespoons olive oil

Zest and juice of 1 lemon

Salt and freshly ground black pepper

6 ounces (170 g) arugula

4 ounces (115 g) soft goat cheese, at room temperature

¼ cup (35 g) toasted pistachios, chopped

Return the reserved 1 cup (240 ml) cooking water to the pan and add the vinegar, sugar, thyme, coriander seeds, fennel seeds, mustard seeds, and allspice. Place over medium-high heat and bring to a boil. Remove from the heat and pour the liquid over the beets. Set aside to pickle for at least 20 minutes or up to 1 hour (or cover and refrigerate overnight). Using a slotted spoon, lift the beets out of the pickling liquid, leaving the spices behind (it's okay if some remain with the beets).

To make the salad:

In a small bowl, whisk the oil with the lemon zest and juice and season with salt and pepper. Place the arugula in a large bowl, add the dressing, and toss to coat. Divide the salad among four plates. Crumble the goat cheese over the arugula and top with the pickled beets. Garnish with the pistachios and serve.

Big Green Bowl Macaroni Salad

4 large eggs

⅓ cup (75 ml) apple cider vinegar

⅓ cup (65 g) sugar

1 tablespoon grainy mustard

1 small yellow onion, grated on the large holes of a box grater

2 tablespoons finely chopped fresh thyme

2 tablespoons finely chopped fresh tarragon

2 tablespoons finely chopped fresh chives

Salt

1 pound (450 g) tricolor rotini pasta

4 medium carrots (about 8 ounces/225 g), peeled, quartered lengthwise, and sliced ¼ inch (6 mm) thick

1 medium cucumber, peeled, quartered, and sliced ¼ inch (6 mm) thick

Zest and juice of 1 lime

¼ cup (60 ml) mayonnaise

Freshly ground black pepper

Growing up near Seneca Lake with a large family meant we had a lot of picnics. At every picnic, Mom would bring a big green bowl filled with macaroni salad that we would share with the family, and at the end of the day we always brought the bowl home empty. My aunts would continually ask my mom for the recipe, and she would always nonchalantly claim, "Oh, it's just macaroni and veggies." But the secret was that Mom would grate the onion into the salad with a box grater. Apparently Dad and us kids didn't like onions, but they were necessary for flavor, so Mom got sneaky. Grating the onion got the flavor of the onion into the salad without danger of us biting into larger pieces.

I've enhanced this recipe by adding beautiful fresh herbs and a splash of lime juice. The herbs add incredible flavor, but the citrus is what magnifies it, adding a wonderful zing to the salad, balancing out the mayonnaise and lightening the dish. For a little extra crunch, Mom sometimes adds radishes—definitely worth a try!

=========== SERVES 6 ===========

First, prepare the eggs: Bring a small pot of water to a boil over medium-high heat. Using a slotted spoon, gently lower the eggs one at a time into the water and boil for 8 minutes. Turn off the heat and let the eggs sit for 4 minutes. Drain the water from the pot and run cold water over the eggs until they're just slightly warm. Peel the eggs underneath the cold water (this helps remove the membrane that's just under the shell of the egg); starting at the bottom of the egg and working your way up makes peeling easier. Chop the eggs into bite-size pieces, place in a bowl, and set aside.

In a small bowl, combine the vinegar, sugar, mustard, onion, thyme, tarragon, and chives and whisk to dissolve the sugar.

Meanwhile, bring a large pot of salted water to a boil, add the pasta, and cook according to the package instructions for al dente. Drain the pasta and transfer it to a large bowl. While the pasta is still warm, pour the vinegar-herb mixture over it and toss to coat (adding the herbs and vinegar while the pasta is warm allows it to absorb the flavor). Set the pasta aside to cool to room temperature, stirring a few times.

Add the carrots, cucumber, and eggs to the cooled pasta. Add the lime zest and juice and mayonnaise, season with salt and pepper, and gently fold to incorporate. Cover and refrigerate until chilled. Serve cold.

Spending time at the lake with my siblings is one of my favorite summertime activities. Here we are at the annual summer solstice party waiting to see the famous "green flash."

Charred Corn and Crispy Chickpea Summer Salad

This is my go-to hot-weather salad: The salty crunch of the chickpeas against the sweetness of the corn, the tang from the lemon, and the juiciness of the tomatoes all scream summer. At any given time in the season, all of these ingredients can be found in my kitchen. This salad makes me want to sit outside with sunshine beating down on me and a cool glass of lemonade in my hand.

The best part about this salad is that there are no rules. Try it once my way, then feel free to adjust the recipe however you like. I bet it would be delicious with some snap peas and radishes added to the mix, and how about peaches? Feel free to get creative!

=========== SERVES 4 ===========

Heat 2 teaspoons of the grapeseed oil in a medium skillet over high heat. Add the corn and cook, stirring frequently, until well charred, about 3 minutes. Season with salt and pepper, transfer to a large bowl, and set aside to cool.

In a small high-sided saucepan, heat the remaining ¼ cup (60 ml) grapeseed oil over high heat and add the chickpeas. Be careful— the oil will splatter; I recommend covering the pan and tossing them often for 3 to 5 minutes, until crisp. Transfer to a paper towel–lined plate, season with salt and pepper, and cool.

In a small bowl, whisk the olive oil into the lemon juice. Add the scallion and season with salt and pepper.

Add the chickpeas, tomato, and lettuce to the bowl with the corn. Add dressing to coat and toss well. Garnish with the cheese and serve.

¼ cup (60 ml) plus 2 teaspoons grapeseed oil

Kernels from 1 ear corn

Salt and freshly ground black pepper

¼ cup (40 g) cooked chickpeas, rinsed and patted dry with a paper towel

¼ cup (60 ml) olive oil

Juice of ½ lemon

1 scallion, thinly sliced

1 ripe tomato, preferably on the vine, cut into wedges

1 head red-leaf lettuce, torn into pieces

2 tablespoons shredded Parmesan cheese

Fried Green Tomatoes
with Basil Aioli

For the green tomatoes

3 large green tomatoes

Salt

1 teaspoon minced fresh ginger

¼ to ½ teaspoon red pepper flakes

1 tablespoon chopped fresh dill

Zest and juice of 1 lemon

⅔ cup (80 g) all-purpose flour

⅔ cup (115 g) medium- or coarse-grained cornmeal

Freshly ground black pepper

1 cup (240 ml) buttermilk

For the aioli

1 large egg yolk

1 small clove garlic

3 large basil leaves

¼ teaspoon salt, or to taste

¼ teaspoon cracked black pepper

Zest and juice of ½ lemon

½ cup (120 ml) olive oil

Vegetable oil, for frying

When my cousin Emily and I were little, we would have epic slumber parties where we would roll our hair, plop ourselves on a pile of pillows in the living room, and watch the movie *Fried Green Tomatoes*. When we would wake up in the morning, our hair would be as curly as Shirley Temple's, and we would call our grandma and ask if she would make us fried green tomatoes for lunch. Lucky for us, Grandma had a garden in her backyard where she grew tomatoes, and she taught us how to make this special dish.

We were probably eight back then, and to this day Emily and I still send each other photos any time we come across fried green tomatoes on a menu. There is a restaurant in Philly that has them, and they're so good that they are almost always sold out. I'm glad my grandma taught me how to make them, so I can eat them anytime, and now you can make them at home, too.

===== SERVES 4 =====

To make the green tomatoes:

Cut a small sliver off either side of the tomatoes (so the batter will stick to all of the slices), then slice them ¼ inch (6 mm) thick. Lay the slices over a 9-by-13-inch (23-by-33-cm) baking dish. Sprinkle the tomatoes with ½ teaspoon salt, the ginger, red pepper flakes, dill, and lemon zest and juice (it's only necessary to season one side). Set aside to marinate while you prepare the aioli (or prep the green tomatoes a day ahead; cover and refrigerate until you're ready to finish the recipe).

To make the aioli:

Combine the egg yolk, garlic, basil, salt, pepper, and lemon zest and juice in a food processor. With the machine running, very slowly drizzle in the olive oil through the hole in the lid until the mixture is emulsified to the consistency of mayonnaise. Transfer the aioli to one large dipping bowl or four individual dipping bowls.

To fry the green tomatoes:

Pour about ½ inch (1.25 cm) of vegetable oil into a high-sided skillet or sauté pan. Place over medium-high heat and heat until the temperature reads 375°F (190°C) on a candy thermometer, or when a pinch of flour bubbles when dropped into the oil.

While the oil is coming up to temperature, in a large bowl, combine the flour and cornmeal and season with salt and pepper; whisk well to incorporate. Pour onto a large plate. Pour the buttermilk over the tomatoes and shift the baking dish back and forth a couple of times to ensure that the tomato slices are evenly coated. Remove the tomato slices one by one, allowing excess liquid to drain, then dredge the slices in the cornmeal mixture to completely coat them. As each tomato slice is soaked and dredged, place it on a baking sheet as you prepare the next (I like to dedicate one hand for the soaking and the other for the dredging to keep things tidy).

Working in two batches, fry the tomato slices for about 3 minutes on each side, using tongs to turn them, until golden brown and crisp all over. Transfer to a paper towel–lined baking sheet and immediately sprinkle with salt. Arrange the fried green tomatoes on a serving plate and serve with the aioli alongside for dipping.

Broccolini and Gruyère Quiche

½ recipe pie crust (see page 163)

6 large eggs

⅓ cup (75 ml) heavy cream

½ teaspoon salt

¼ teaspoon cracked black pepper

1 cup (100 g) shredded Gruyère cheese

12 ounces (340 g) broccolini (1 small bunch), chopped

1 small yellow onion, very thinly sliced

1 tablespoon chopped fresh parsley

1 tablespoon fresh chives, cut into 1-inch (2.5-cm) batons, plus 1 teaspoon finely chopped fresh chives

Until I was about twelve, you could not get me to eat quiche. The idea of eating an "egg pie" seemed so strange to me. A class trip to Quebec changed my mind, and now I love it. The wonderful thing about quiche is that you can put just about anything in it! I like making quiche on the weekends, as it allows me to clean out my fridge, fill up my stomach, and let nothing go to waste. For the fancy effect, pair your quiche with an authentic French mixed greens salad with mustard vinaigrette and eat it on your prettiest plate.

If you're worried about what to do with the other half of your pie dough, you can wrap it tightly in plastic and put it in the freezer; when you're ready to use it, let it come to room temperature before rolling it out. Alternatively, you can simply halve the pie recipe so there are no leftovers.

SERVES 8

Preheat the oven to 375°F (190°C).

Roll out the pie dough according to the directions on page 163 to fit a 9-inch (23-cm) glass pie plate. Chill in the refrigerator while you prepare your ingredients.

In a large bowl, whisk together the eggs, cream, salt, and pepper and add the cheese (the liquid from the eggs suspends the cheese so it doesn't fall to the bottom of the pan). In a separate bowl, combine the broccolini, onion, and parsley and place in the pie crust. Pour the egg mixture over the broccolini mixture and top with the chives. Place on the middle rack of the oven; to catch any potential spills if your quiche bubbles over, place a baking sheet on the lowest rack. Bake for 35 to 40 minutes, until the eggs are set. A helpful trick to check for doneness is to look up through the bottom of the pie plate. If you see any wet spots, it means your pie crust is not fully cooked and you should return it to the oven in 5-minute increments. Cool on a cooling rack and serve warm or at room temperature.

Duck Confit

¼ cup (35 g) coarse salt

1 medium shallot, thinly sliced

4 cloves garlic, smashed and peeled

1 teaspoon cracked black pepper

6 sprigs fresh thyme

4 duck legs, with thighs attached

4 duck wings

1 bay leaf

About 4½ cups (1 L) duck fat

Duck confit is one of the most indulgent recipes I can think of. It's time-consuming to make, but as long as your confit is sealed properly, it will keep for up to six months. The idea behind confit is that before refrigeration was invented, this was a way to preserve food through the long winter. The duck is cooked so slowly that as its fat melts, it begins to cover the meat, and once the meat is cooked completely, the fat will solidify as it returns to room temperature, creating a barrier where bacteria cannot grow.

I've included this recipe to make this indulgent treat more accessible for people who have never attempted confit before. But if you have some experience with the dish and are feeling brave, my suggestion is to purchase a whole duck, break it down, prepare the breasts for dinner (see page 133), make stock with the body, and render the body fat separately to confit the wings and thighs. Then you can reuse the fat for poutine (page 86) anytime you like. It's a lot of work for two thighs and wings, but it's well worth it.

===== SERVES 4 =====

Sprinkle half of the salt on the bottom of a container large enough to hold the duck pieces in a single layer. Scatter half each of the shallot, garlic, pepper, and thyme in the dish and layer the duck legs and wings, skin side up, on top. Sprinkle with the remaining salt, shallot, garlic, pepper, and thyme and top with the bay leaf. Cover the dish and refrigerate for at least 24 hours or, preferably, up to 2 days.

Preheat the oven to 225°F (105°C).

Remove the duck from the container and rinse off the salt and seasonings with cold water. Thoroughly pat dry with paper towels. Transfer to an ovenproof dish just large enough to hold the pieces in an even layer. Spoon the duck fat over the legs, thighs, and wings; as it melts, it will cover the meat evenly.

Place the dish in the oven. When the fat is fully melted, cover the dish with aluminum foil and cook the duck for at least 3 hours and up to 6 hours. As long as the temperature remains low so the fat doesn't boil, you can potentially keep the duck in the oven all day.

Remove the dish from the oven and cool. Store the duck, completely immersed in the fat, in a container in the refrigerator for at least 3 days and up to 6 months before serving. Serve warm or cold, with a light salad and toasts, if you like.

THE DISH:
The Diner Takeover challenge felt really familiar to me because it was just like working in my family's pizza shop. I often hopped between stations, alternating the role of "fryer queen" and "deli girl," so I had no problem feeling comfortable in this challenge. When it was time to begin the challenge and we were handed the paper diner hats, I started laughing because my grandmother has boxes of them in her basement! She told me later that when the episode aired she pulled out a box and made everyone wear one while they watched.

Duck Fat Poutine

2 (1-pound/450-g) russet potatoes

For the gravy

2 tablespoons unsalted butter

3 tablespoons all-purpose flour

2 cups (480 ml) duck or chicken stock

Salt and freshly ground black pepper

For frying and assembling

2 cups (480 ml) duck fat

2 cups (300 g) cheese curds

Poutine—french fries fried in duck fat, topped with cheese curds, and smothered in gravy—is basically the best bar food you will ever eat. Make a dish of this for Game Day and you won't care who wins or loses. If you want to take this recipe to the next level (trust me, you do), I'd highly recommend topping it with some of the duck confit (page 84) you've been storing in the back of the fridge. Just peel the meat off the bone and heat it in a small pan before adding it to the poutine.

====== SERVES 4 TO 6 ======

Scrub the potatoes with a vegetable brush under cold running water. Cut the potatoes into 4-by-½-inch (10-by-1.25-cm) french fry shapes. Place in a bowl filled with cold water (doing so prevents browning) while you prepare the gravy.

To make the gravy:
In a small saucepan, melt the butter over medium heat. Add the flour and cook, whisking constantly, until the flour turns lightly golden and is slightly thickened, about 2 minutes. Whisk in the stock and continue whisking constantly until thickened to a gravy, dissolving any lumps, about 2 minutes. Season with salt and pepper, turn off the heat, and cover with a lid to keep warm.

To fry the potatoes and assemble:
Remove the potatoes from the water and dry thoroughly with paper towels (if they aren't dried properly, they will splatter). Heat the duck fat in a shallow sauté pan over medium-high heat until a candy thermometer reads 350°F (175°C). Working in batches, add the potatoes without crowding the pan and fry until golden brown, about 7 minutes. Using a slotted spoon, transfer to a paper towel–lined plate and sprinkle with salt. Plate the poutine by layering fries, cheese curds, and gravy into four to six small bowls (or a single large dish, if you like). Serve immediately.

Shrimp Cocktail

When I was growing up, nearly every social gathering my mom hosted featured shrimp cocktail, as it was her favorite. She would dress it up by serving it in martini glasses with some ice and lettuce, with the shrimp hanging off the rim of the glass. Cleaning and preparing shrimp is not something to fear; it's surprisingly easy to do, and once you learn, you'll never buy peeled and deveined shrimp again. The first time I cleaned a shrimp, I was in the Italian Market in Philly, and I asked the fishmonger for a demonstration; if you ask at your fish market, I'll bet they'd be happy to show you, too.

=============== SERVES 4 TO 6 ===============

Fill a large bowl with ice and water and set aside. Bring a medium pot of salted water to boil and add the shrimp. Boil for 1 to 2 minutes, until the shrimp are vibrant pink and white and the tails curl to the heads. Drain the shrimp and plunge them into the ice water to chill completely.

In a small bowl, combine the ketchup or chile sauce (or a little bit of both, if you're feeling creative!), the lemon juice, and horseradish and season with salt.

Fill four to six cocktail glasses halfway with crushed ice and cover the ice with a lettuce leaf, if desired. Pour the cocktail sauce evenly over the lettuce, hang the shrimp on the rims of the glasses, and serve.

Salt

1 pound (450 g) jumbo shrimp, peeled and deveined, with the tails left on

½ cup (120 ml) ketchup or guajillo chile sauce (see page 90)

½ teaspoon fresh lemon juice

2 tablespoons finely grated fresh horseradish or 1 tablespoon bottled horseradish

4 to 6 iceberg lettuce leaves, for garnish (optional)

Deviled Eggs

Deviled eggs have somehow gotten a bum rap. But why? They're always a hit! Straying only slightly from the classic recipe, I like to top mine with crispy pancetta and fresh chives to bring a little extra crunch, salt, and herbaceous flavor. And switching out the traditional mayonnaise for tangy sour cream is a great way to lighten the dish. This recipe is simple enough that if you keep a couple hard-boiled eggs in the fridge, you're only five minutes away from a delicious lunch.

If you plan to serve these at a cocktail party, here's a little tip: Arrange the deviled eggs on a dish in no particular pattern or shape so when they disappear one by one your dish won't look dismantled. And putting them on a vintage platter will make their color pop—they'll be a real standout.

6 large eggs

3 slices pancetta

2 tablespoons sour cream

1 tablespoon grainy mustard

¼ teaspoon apple cider vinegar

¼ teaspoon salt

¼ teaspoon paprika

1 teaspoon thinly sliced fresh chives

===== MAKES 12 DEVILED EGGS =====

Bring a medium pot of water to boil over medium-high heat. Using a slotted spoon, gently lower the eggs one at a time into the water and boil for 8 minutes. Turn off the heat and let the eggs sit for 4 minutes. Drain the water from the pot and run cold water over the eggs until they're just slightly warm. Peel the eggs underneath the cold water (this helps remove the membrane that's just under the shell of the egg); starting at the bottom of the egg and working your way up makes peeling easier. Pat dry with paper towels.

While the eggs are boiling, in a large skillet, cook the pancetta over medium heat until crisped on both sides, about 5 minutes. Transfer to a paper towel–lined plate to cool, then break into bite-size pieces.

Cut the eggs in half lengthwise. Carefully transfer the whites to a plate and the yolks to a medium bowl. Add the sour cream, mustard, vinegar, salt, and paprika to the bowl with the yolks and combine, breaking up the yolks with a fork and stirring until smooth.

Using a teaspoon or a pastry bag fitted with a star tip, fill the whites with the yolk mixture. Arrange the eggs on a platter, top each with a piece of pancetta, garnish with the chives, and serve.

Crispy Pigs' Ears with Dandelion and Fennel Salad and Quail Eggs

For the pigs' ears

4 pigs' ears

1 yellow onion, cut in half

2 tablespoons whole pink or black peppercorns

4 bay leaves

For the chile sauce

3 dried guajillo chiles, seeds removed

3 tablespoons red wine vinegar

1 clove garlic, peeled

3 tablespoons brown sugar

1 tablespoon olive oil

For the relish

Zest and juice of 2 limes

Zest and juice of 1 lemon

2 tablespoons olive oil

Salt and freshly ground black pepper

1 Persian cucumber, or ½ English cucumber, finely diced

½ fennel bulb, cored and finely diced, fronds picked and reserved

When I made this dish in the *MasterChef* Finale, I wanted to send a clear message that I was taking risks, not playing it safe. My inspiration came from a dish I had eaten at a restaurant in Los Angeles called Animal; they fried their pigs' ears after braising them for thirty hours. There was no way I could create the same texture and flavor as theirs in the one hour I was given; my mission was simply to prove that I had the ability to take unwanted ingredients and make them into something luxurious, something the judges wouldn't have expected.

This is the recipe that opened my finale meal—try it, and you'll be surprised how delicious pigs' ears are. Just a little tip: Pigs' ears usually require a special order at your local butcher, and the quail eggs that are served on top can be found in specialty groceries and Asian markets. And if you're ever in Los Angeles, stop by Animal and try the dish that inspired mine.

======================= SERVES 4 =======================

To make the pigs' ears:
In a pressure cooker, combine the pigs' ears, onion, peppercorns, bay leaves, and enough water to generously cover the ingredients. Securely close the cooker and cook at high pressure for 30 minutes, then turn off the heat and let the pressure cooker depressurize naturally. Meanwhile, prepare the chile sauce, relish, and salad.

To make the chile sauce:
In a bowl, soak the guajillo chiles in enough hot water to cover for about 10 minutes, until softened. Drain. In a blender, combine the chiles, vinegar, garlic, brown sugar, and oil and blend until smooth.

To make the relish:

In a medium bowl, combine the lime juice, lemon juice, and oil and season with salt and pepper. In a separate medium bowl, combine the cucumber, fennel and fennel fronds, apple, celeriac, and jalapeño and Fresno chiles. Add all but 2 tablespoons of the dressing (reserve it to dress the salad) and toss to coat the vegetables.

To make the salad:

In a large bowl, combine the dandelion greens, fennel, and cucumber. Add the sugar to the 2 tablespoons reserved dressing from the relish and toss with the salad.

To fry the pigs' ears:

Fill a large bowl with ice and weater. Remove the pigs' ears from the braising liquid in the pressure cooker and immediately transfer to the ice bath to stop the cooking. Remove from the water and pat dry with paper towels (the ears will retain a lot of water from cooking and will splatter quite a bit in the fryer if they aren't dried thoroughly; if you have a splash guard or a lid, use it) and slice into ¼-inch (6-mm) strips. Add 2 inches (5 cm) of oil to a large sauté pan and heat over medium-high heat until a candy thermometer reads 375°F (190°C). Pour the flour into a shallow bowl and season generously with salt and pepper. Dredge the strips in the flour, shake off the excess, and deep-fry for 5 to 6 minutes, until browned and crisp. Transfer to a paper towel–lined plate.

To serve:

Place one-quarter of the salad and one-quarter of the relish side by side on a plate. Top the salad with a sliced pig's ear and top the pig's ear with a quail egg. Garnish the plate with a smear of the chile sauce. Repeat with the remaining ingredients to fill four plates.

½ Granny Smith apple, cored and finely diced

¼ cup finely diced peeled celeriac

1 jalapeño chile, seeded and finely diced

2 Fresno chiles, seeded and finely diced

For the salad

1 bunch dandelion greens, torn into bite-size pieces

¼ fennel bulb, shaved lengthwise with a vegetable peeler or on a mandoline

1 Persian cucumber, or ½ English cucumber, shaved with a vegetable peeler or on a mandoline

Pinch of sugar

2 tablespoons reserved dressing from the relish

For frying and serving

Vegetable oil

1½ cups (200 g) quick-mixing flour, such as Wondra

Salt and freshly ground black pepper

4 quail eggs, cooked sunny side up

Chicken Salad

For the dressing

1 tablespoon olive oil

1 small shallot, finely diced

1 tablespoon apple cider vinegar

2 teaspoons sugar

¼ cup (60 ml) Greek yogurt, plus more if you like your chicken salad creamier

1 tablespoon poppy seeds, toasted

¼ teaspoon salt

For the chicken salad

1 (3-pound/1.4-kg) rotisserie chicken, skin removed, meat picked into bite-size pieces

1 cup (65 g) chopped celery

1 cup (90 g) mixed green and red grapes, cut in half

1 seedless cucumber, cut in half lengthwise and sliced

1 green apple, cored and cut into ½-inch (1.25-cm) pieces

1 shallot, diced

2 teaspoons chopped fresh chives

2 teaspoons chopped fresh parsley

2 teaspoons chopped fresh tarragon

Salt and freshly cracked black pepper

¼ cup (20 g) toasted sliced almonds

I don't know about you, but I like my chicken salad on the sweeter side. Tossed with grapes, apple, celery, and poppy seed dressing and served on cranberry toast, it's the perfect pick-me-up halfway through the day. You can also enjoy it with crackers, in a pita pocket, or in lettuce leaf cups—it's low-maintenance and travels easily. I use a mixture of white and dark meat; the dark meat brings incredible moisture and flavor to the salad. In this recipe, I call for a rotisserie chicken that you can purchase at your grocery store; it definitely saves you time, but if you'd rather roast your own chicken (see page 130), feel free!

=========== SERVES 4 TO 6 ===========

To make the dressing:

In a small sauté pan, heat the oil over medium-low heat. Add the shallot and without allowing it to color, cook until translucent, about 2 minutes. Transfer to a small bowl. Add the vinegar, sugar, yogurt, and poppy seeds and whisk to combine.

To make the chicken salad:

In a large bowl, combine the chicken meat, celery, grapes, cucumber, apple, shallot, chives, parsley, and tarragon. Season with salt and pepper.

Add the dressing and toss to coat. Top with toasted almonds and serve.

Fried Herbes de Provence Sweetbreads over Vegetable Pot au Feu

For the sweetbreads

1 pound (450 g) sweetbreads

3 cups (720 ml) milk

2 bay leaves

3 tablespoons apple cider vinegar

For the pot au feu

1 shallot, roughly chopped

3 sprigs fresh thyme

4 small Red Bliss potatoes, quartered

2 baby fennel bulbs, quartered, or 1 regular fennel bulb, cut into eighths

1 small head purple cauliflower, cut into florets (white or yellow is okay, too)

8 baby carrots, cut in half lengthwise

¼ cup (25 g) baby Brussels sprouts

4 asparagus stalks, woody ends snapped off, cut into 1-inch (2.5-cm) pieces

¼ cup (20 g) sugar snap peas

Salt and freshly ground black pepper

I went back and forth deciding whether I would include bulls' testicles in this book. Bulls' testicles was the dish that secured my spot in the final four, and I was proud of it because it sent a strong message to my competitors that I would tackle whatever was thrown at me. In the end I decided that if I were to follow through, this would most likely be a recipe that very few would attempt to make. Not only are the actual testicles difficult to come by, but how many people would really want to make them? So I swapped in sweetbreads.

Sweetbreads, the thymus gland of a calf, are now considered a delicacy. When prepared properly, sweetbreads are sometimes described as "fancy chicken nuggets." They are soaked in milk overnight to remove any blood and metallic taste, and then they are parboiled or blanched, following which an outer membrane is removed before cooking them. Once I got home from filming, I was excited to try this dish with a different, but still delicious, protein.

I first learned about pot au feu from David Tanis's book *One Good Dish*. His was made with all vegetables—you would start with a broth, add your heartier vegetables such as potatoes, then add another smaller vegetable every few minutes, until you finished with a handful of fresh peas that only needed a minute to cook. The whole preparation is very relaxed, with no strict time frame as to when you should add the next component. It's mostly done by instinct, much like making a soup. I remember thinking, "Here's something I can do when I don't really know what to do," and it sure did come in handy.

═══════════════ SERVES 4 ═══════════════

To make the sweetbreads:

Place the sweetbreads in a bowl and add the milk (make sure the milk covers the sweetbreads completely, so depending on the size of your container, you may need to add more milk), loosely cover, and soak for 8 to 10 hours in the refrigerator (this draws out blood and takes away the metallic taste). After soaking, the sweetbreads will have turned white and the milk will have become pink. Drain and discard the milk. In a large saucepan, combine 4 cups (1 L) water, the bay leaves, and vinegar and bring to a boil over high heat. Add the sweetbreads, reduce the heat, and simmer for 15 minutes, then drain. Meanwhile, fill a large bowl with ice and water. Transfer the sweetbreads to the ice-water bath to shock them and stop the cooking. Once they are cooled, use your fingertips to peel off the membrane surrounding the sweetbreads; as you do so, the sweetbreads will break apart into smaller bite-size pieces—set them aside in a bowl while you make the pot au feu.

To make the pot au feu:

While the sweetbreads are blanching, in a large saucepan, combine 3 cups (720 ml) water, the shallot, and thyme and bring to a boil over medium heat. Add the potatoes, cover, and cook for 6 minutes. Add the fennel, cover, and cook for another 6 minutes. Add the cauliflower, cover, and cook for 5 minutes. Add the carrots, cover, and cook for 4 minutes. Add the Brussels sprouts, cover and cook for 4 minutes. Add the asparagus, cover, and cook for 4 minutes. Finally, add the snap peas, cover, and cook for 4 minutes. The water level in the pot will lower significantly, but there is no need to stir because the steam created in the pot will cook the smaller vegetables on top. After the snap peas are cooked, remove the pot from the heat, season generously with salt and pepper, and move on to frying the sweetbreads.

To fry the sweetbreads:

In a small bowl, whisk the eggs with a pinch of salt and set aside. Put ½ cup (62 g) of the flour into a shallow bowl and season with salt

Recipe continues

For frying the sweetbreads

2 large eggs, beaten

Salt

1 cup (125 g) all-purpose flour

Freshly ground black pepper

½ cup (80 g) yellow cornmeal

1 tablespoon herbes de Provence

2 tablespoons (60 ml) grapeseed oil

For the sauce

1 tablespoon grainy mustard

1 tablespoon fresh lemon juice

1 tablespoon olive oil

For the garnish

2 asparagus stalks, woody ends snapped off, thinly sliced with a vegetable peeler or on a mandoline

2 breakfast radishes, stems trimmed, thinly sliced with a vegetable peeler or on a mandoline

and pepper. In a third bowl, combine the remaining ½ cup (62 g) flour, the cornmeal, and herbes de Provence. Using one hand designated for dry ingredients and one for wet, dredge the sweetbread pieces in the flour, then in the egg mixture, and finally in the cornmeal-herb mixture.

In a large skillet over medium heat, heat 1 tablespoon of the grapeseed oil. Add half of the sweetbreads and swirl the pan so the oil catches on each piece and fry, turning once, until golden brown all over, 1 to 2 minutes per side. Remove with a slotted spoon, transfer to a paper towel–lined plate, and season with salt. Add the remaining 1 tablespoon oil to the pan and repeat to fry the second batch of sweetbreads.

To make the sauce:

In a small bowl, whisk the mustard and lemon juice into the olive oil.

To serve:

Divide the pot au feu vegetables into the centers of four plates. Top with the fried sweetbreads and drizzle each plate with about a teaspoon of mustard sauce. Garnish with the shaved asparagus and radishes and serve.

Blood Orange Mimosas

This twist on a traditional mimosa is a great way to punch up a common brunch drink. The blood orange not only gives the mimosa a great, bright color, but it creates an intense citrus flavor—not to mention the fact that using freshly squeezed juice adds a refreshing kick to this classic. There is nothing that makes me feel fancier than raising a glass of this cocktail and toasting with my friends.

3 to 4 medium blood oranges

1 (750-ml) bottle champagne or sparkling wine, chilled

=== SERVES 8 ===

Using a vegetable peeler, peel 8 vertical strips from the blood oranges. Gently squeeze each strip over a glass to release their oils, then drop one into each glass. Squeeze the blood oranges to make 1 cup (240 ml) juice. Add 2 tablespoons of the juice to each glass, top with champagne to fill the glasses, and serve.

I've loved citrus since I was about three. Oranges, grapefruits, and lemons carry the perfect balance of sweetness and tang that I've always enjoyed, even as a little girl. Here I am helping my uncle by picking the prettiest lemons for him to juice.

Pop-up Picnic Lunch

A bottle of bubbly is an easy way to take a brown bag lunch and turn it into an elegant picnic. I'm lucky to have been given my great-grandmother's picnic basket—which I pack with a soft blanket, a deck of playing cards, and antique silverware and plates. Pair this with a good book and a few champagne glasses, and you're on your way to a memorable afternoon with friends or loved ones. Squeeze the blood oranges into a Mason jar at home to make for easy travel, and plan your menu around things that can stand the heat of the sun. Bonus points if you bring an instrument or a friend who can play one.

Dinner

THE RECIPES

In my family, dinner has always been the daily "check in."

Everyone shares their highs, and sometimes their lows, and it's the time of the day that requires you to slow down and enjoy being with those around you.

When I was growing up, the question of "what's for dinner" was called throughout my house starting immediately after school. While we completed our homework, we all waited to hear Dad's car come up the driveway, signaling that dinner was going to start soon. We would each share a little bit about our day while we ate, and after we were finished, we would all clean up together.

I have so many memories with my family surrounding the dinner table, and it's my goal to have these recipes be a part of your family time as well.

Simple Chicken Stock

Trim and bones from 1 chicken

2 tablespoons olive oil

2 medium unpeeled yellow onions, quartered (the skins will add lovely color)

2 celery stalks, cut into large pieces

2 medium carrots, cut into large pieces

1 medium fennel bulb, quartered

2 bay leaves

1 tablespoon whole black peppercorns

2 cloves garlic

4 sprigs fresh thyme

1 sprig fresh rosemary

Salt to taste

Filtered water

A good stock is the base to any delicious soup. Once you learn how easy it is to make your own, you'll be cooking soup all the time. Save the ends and "scraps" of vegetables when you cook, add them into the stockpot with your chicken bones, and you're sure to have a flavorful stock every time.

Make this stock by saving the chicken bones from Roast Chicken with Lemon and Olives (page 130) and use it for Italian Wedding Soup (opposite page) or wherever else stock is called for. Stock freezes well, so "stock" up and stay warm all winter long.

===== MAKES ABOUT 8 CUPS (2 L) =====

Heat the oil in a large stockpot over medium heat. Add the onions and cook until very dark all over, about 2 minutes on each side. Add the celery, carrots, and fennel and sear for a minute or two to color them as well. Add the remaining ingredients and just enough filtered water to cover. Increase the heat to high, bring to a boil, then reduce the heat, cover, and simmer for at least 1 hour or up to 2 hours. Strain through a fine-mesh sieve into a heatproof bowl, and your stock is ready to be used in your recipes. Store for up to 7 days in the refrigerator or 6 months in the freezer.

Italian Wedding Soup

Growing up, I always loved soup. Whether it was Grandma's pasta e fagioli, chicken noodle, or hearty lentil, I would eat it in a huge bowl and savor every spoonful. For a long time, I would eat canned soup because it was so cheap; my favorite was the "chickarina" style because it had mini meatballs in it. When I finally learned how to make my own stock, I realized just how easy it can be to make soup from scratch. The whole idea is to build your flavors in layers and take your time; cooking soup over low heat for a long time is the key to flavorful results. When Grandma makes this soup, she puts the meatballs in raw, letting them cook slowly in the broth; I prefer to give the meatballs a good sear first so they look more vibrant in the broth. If you want to include a childhood throwback, use little pasta stars in place of the acini di pepe.

═══════════ SERVES 4 ═══════════

6 cups (1.4 L) Simple Chicken Stock (opposite page)

3 medium carrots, thinly sliced

3 celery stalks, cut in half lengthwise and sliced ¼ inch (6 mm) thick

3 Italian sausage links (about 4 ounces/115 g each), casings removed

½ cup (50 g) acini di pepe or other small pasta shape

¼ cup (15 g) thickly sliced scallion greens (about ¼-inch/6-mm slices)

2 cups (60 g) baby spinach

Crusty bread, for serving (optional)

In a large saucepan over high heat, bring the broth to a simmer. Add the carrots and celery, reduce the heat to low, and simmer for 10 minutes.

Meanwhile, put the sausage in a small bowl and shape it into about twenty 1-inch (2.5-cm) meatballs. Heat a large skillet over high heat and sear the meatballs for about 30 seconds on each side to give them some good color. Place the meatballs in the broth, where they will finish cooking and add incredible flavor to the soup.

Add the acini di pepe and cover. Continue to cook the soup over extremely low heat until the acini di pepe is cooked through and doubled in size. This could take a while (at most 30 minutes), but it is building flavor that would otherwise not develop if rushed. Add the scallions and spinach and cook until just wilted, 1 to 2 minutes. Spoon into bowls and serve with some crusty bread alongside for dunking, if you like.

Lapresi's Pizza

For the pizza dough

1⅓ cups warm water (105°F to 115°F/40°C to 45°C)

1 tablespoon sugar

1 (¼-ounce/7-g) packet active dry yeast

3½ cups (435 g) all-purpose flour, plus more for dusting

1 tablespoon salt

2 tablespoons olive oil

2 tablespoons cornmeal

For the toppings

About 1 cup (240 ml) tomato sauce (page 110)

About 8 ounces (225 g) shredded mozzarella cheese

48 slices pepperoni (about 7 ounces/200 g)

8 cremini mushrooms, each cut into 4 slices

2 (4-ounce/115-g) Italian sausage links, casings removed

My first-ever experience in a kitchen was in my family's restaurant, Lapresi's Pizza Emporium and Deli. In its early years, my grandfather bought the building and ran it as a grocery store; when the store became the pizza shop, my grandfather also developed a business distributing pizza supplies throughout the state. When he got older, he passed the pizza run to my uncle and the shop to my aunt. As the grandkids got older, we all took a turn working in the pizza shop. But something we were never allowed to do was make the pizzas. You see, there was a very specific way of assembling the toppings. Because my grandpa lived through the Great Depression and served in World War II, we were not allowed to waste anything. Each pepperoni was to be counted out and placed on the pizza in a pattern according to what size you were making. His method worked so that each bite had an appropriate topping and no topping was wasted. It's the only way I knew pizza to be, and I am happy to share it with you.

This recipe is for our most popular pizza—pepperoni, mushroom, and sausage—but you are more than welcome to make your pizza with whatever toppings you like. The recipe makes enough dough for two pizzas; pizza dough freezes well, so you can save the second half for later, if you like. For the full Lapresi experience, use the second half of the dough to make some fried dough (page 180).

=========== MAKES 2 (12-inch/30-cm) PIZZAS ===========

To make the pizza dough:

In a large bowl, combine the water and sugar and sprinkle the yeast on top. In a separate bowl, whisk together the flour and salt. Once the yeast is dissolved and the mixture begins to foam, about 5 minutes, add the oil. Using a wooden spoon, stir the flour into the yeast mixture, in three additions, until the mixture appears well blended and looks shaggy. Transfer the dough to a well-floured work surface and knead, pulling the dough toward you with your fingertips and

Recipe continues

away with the heels of your palms and turning the dough a quarter turn each time you knead, until the dough is fairly smooth (there may be a few ridges remaining, which is fine, but you don't want any lumps or dry flour) and elastic. Transfer the dough to a lightly oiled bowl and cover with plastic wrap. Place in a warm area free of drafts and allow to rise for 1½ hours, or until doubled in volume.

To assemble and bake the pizza:
Preheat the oven to 475°F (245°C) and dust a round pizza sheet (if you don't have a pizza sheet, you can use a baking sheet) with half of the cornmeal.

Take the dough out of the bowl and place it on a well-floured work surface. Knead the dough about 4 times, then divide the dough in half. To make one pizza at a time, stretch half of the dough into a 12-inch (30-cm) circle. Spread ½ cup (120 ml) of the sauce over the dough (you'll know that the sauce is evenly distributed when you squint your eyes and you can't see the dough through the sauce), leaving a 1-inch (2.5-cm) space to form the crust. Sprinkle the cheese over the sauce, using the squinting-eyes trick to make sure the cheese is evenly distributed. To make your pizza in the authentic Lapresi style, arrange the pepperoni so each slice of pizza has 3 pieces, as shown. Add 2 mushroom slices per pizza slice to cover the pepperoni. Sprinkle the sausage evenly over the entire pizza. The goal is to get a taste of each topping in each bite.

Bake the pizza for 12 to 15 minutes, until the bottom is golden brown and the cheese is bubbling. (While the pizza is baking, top your second pizza.) Remove from the oven and cut the pizza into 8 slices, using the pepperoni as a guide (this is why we decorated the pizza the way we did).

P.S. If you slice through the pepperoni, my grandfather will come to your house and scold you and my grandmother will grow another gray hair.

Napoleon-Style Lasagna

2 tablespoons olive oil

1 medium yellow onion, chopped

2 cloves garlic, smashed and peeled

1 teaspoon salt, or to taste

1 (32-ounce/900-g) can crushed San Marzano tomatoes

2 bay leaves

7 to 10 sprigs fresh thyme

Freshly ground black pepper

1 sprig fresh basil

For the lasagna

Salt

1 (16-ounce/450-g) package lasagna sheets

3 cups (740 g) whole-milk ricotta cheese

2 large eggs

Zest of 1 lemon

1 teaspoon chopped fresh thyme

1 teaspoon chopped fresh parsley

1 teaspoon chopped fresh

My grandma had two rules for us while she was working in the kitchen and we were keeping her company: Pull your hair back, and don't touch anything. There was one momentous occasion when all of the Lapresi girls went to Grandma's house so she could teach us how to make lasagna. Upon our arrival, we were given a *mopina* (bandana) and were told to promptly pull our hair back. My grandma turned on the most hilariously quintessential Italian soundtrack, and the seven of us threw on our vintage aprons and got flour everywhere. Our end result was a lasagna and sauce so delicious that we could barely resist eating all of it immediately. With bits of flour still in our hair, we each brought a fair amount home and shared it with our families for dinner. Singing "That's Amore" and taking turns stirring the sauce with the infamous wooden spoon that Grandma would threaten us with if we were in trouble are the kinds of memories I hope to share with my own family one day. But for now, I will share this one with you.

The way I've always built lasagna will result in a beautiful, multilayered lasagna that resembles a layered cake like a napoleon. Simply layer each lasagna sheet with the sauce and cheeses instead of using the casserole-style approach. Feel free to try it this way, or if you prefer it, stick to the casserole-style method. If my cousins and I were able to sing and play around the kitchen while making lasagna, you can too. An extra pinch of basil or salt here and there will personalize the dish. Trust your gut, taste all of your components, and, most important, make this dish with and for the people you love.

===== SERVES 6 TO 8 =====

To make the tomato sauce:

In a large sauté pan, heat the oil over medium heat. Add the onion, garlic, and salt and cook, stirring frequently, until they take on a deep caramel color and become very soft, about 15 minutes. Add the crushed tomatoes, bay leaves, and thyme. Reduce the heat to low, cover, and simmer for 1 hour. Uncover, remove the bay leaves and thyme sprigs, and season with salt and pepper. Transfer to a blender and blend until smooth. Transfer the blended sauce to a bowl or container and add the basil. Steep for 5 minutes, then remove the basil (if you leave it in for too long, it will turn the sauce bitter). Set aside the sauce until ready to assemble.

oregano

Freshly ground black pepper

3 cups (340 g) grated mozzarella cheese

½ cup (60 g) grated Parmesan cheese

To make the lasagna:

Bring a large pot of salted water to a boil. Fill a large bowl with ice and water and set aside. Add the lasagna to the boiling water and cook until slightly under al dente, 3 to 5 minutes for fresh pasta, 10 to 12 minutes for dried pasta (it will continue to cook in the oven). Drain the pasta through a colander, then plunge the pasta into the ice water bath to keep it from overcooking. Drain, pat off excess water with paper towels or a clean dish towel, and lay the pasta flat on a baking sheet, ready to be layered.

Meanwhile, preheat the oven to 375°F (190°C).

In a medium bowl, combine the ricotta, eggs, lemon zest, thyme, parsley, and oregano and season with salt and pepper.

Spread a small amount of the tomato sauce onto the bottom of a 9-by-13-inch (23-by-33-cm) ovenproof dish, leaving a 2- to 3-inch (5- to 7.5-cm) border around the sides (this is what makes the lasagna napoleon style!). Begin building the lasagna, starting with a layer of pasta, then sauce, ricotta mixture, mozzarella, and Parmesan. Continue building until you've used up all the ingredients, finishing with a top layer of sauce and what's left of the mozzarella and Parmesan cheeses. Feel free to make your lasagna more saucy, more cheesy, or however you prefer— this is meant to be a fun dish you can make with your family.

Spray a sheet of aluminum foil with cooking spray; cover the dish with the foil, sprayed side down, and bake for 30 minutes, then remove the foil and continue to bake uncovered for 15 minutes more, or until bubbling. Let rest for 15 minutes before serving.

Ricotta Gnocchi in Brown Butter Sage Sauce

This is the dish that won me my white apron—and not just any white apron, but the first one of the competition!

Gnocchi was always a staple in our house while I was growing up, and I have memories of my siblings and me running through the house screaming "gnocchi and sauce!" when Mom asked what we wanted for dinner. Juggling five kids, dance classes, sports practices, and housework, my mother usually opted for store-bought frozen gnocchi, and we gobbled them up with red sauce and garlic bread at least once a week. Using frozen gnocchi made it easier for us to "help" Mom make dinner. She'd always say, "When they float, you know they're done."

When I made this simple dish in the *MasterChef* kitchen, I stepped it up by adding lemon zest and English peas and lightly searing the gnocchi in a hot pan. I thought of Chef Ramsay saying in past seasons of *MasterChef*, "Color means flavor!" while repeating Mom's gnocchi-cooking advice to myself to keep focused.

When time was called, I felt a surge of pride and I thought of his wise words. I knew that apron was mine!

===== SERVES 4 (Makes about 36 gnocchi) =====

To make the gnocchi:
In a large bowl, mix the ricotta, eggs, Parmesan cheese, salt, and flour with a spoon until just incorporated into a soft dough. Do not overwork the dough or your gnocchi will become tough.

On a well-floured work surface, shape the dough into two ropes that are 1 inch (2.5 cm) in diameter and about 18 inches (46 cm) long (see photos 1 and 2 on page 114). Use the back of a floured butter knife to

Recipe continues

For the gnocchi

8 ounces (225 g) whole-milk ricotta cheese

2 large eggs, beaten

½ cup (60 g) grated Parmesan cheese, plus more for topping

½ teaspoon salt, plus more as needed

1 cup (125 g) all-purpose flour, plus more for dusting

For the sauce

4 tablespoons (½ stick/55 g) unsalted butter

3 or 4 fresh sage leaves

½ cup (65 g) frozen peas, thawed

1 tablespoon fresh lemon zest

Salt and freshly ground black pepper

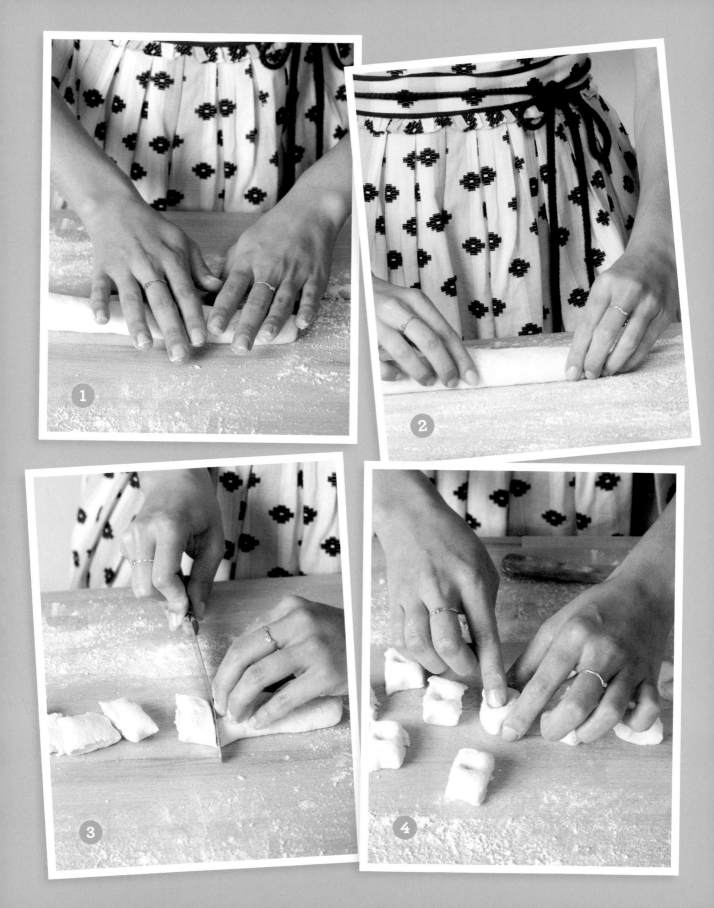

cut the ropes (see photo 3 on page 114) into 1-inch (2.5-cm) pieces. With the tip of your index finger, make a small indentation in each gnocchi (see photo 4 on page 114)—this will allow the gnocchi to best grab hold of the sauce.

Bring a large pot of salted water to a boil. Add the gnocchi in small batches and boil each batch for 2 to 3 minutes, until they float to the top. As the gnocchi are cooked, remove them with a slotted spoon and place in a colander to drain.

Frozen peas aren't just for boo-boos! I've loved them since I was a baby.

To make the sauce:

While the gnocchi are cooking, melt the butter in a small skillet over medium-high heat. Add the sage leaves and continue cooking until the butter begins to brown, about 2 minutes, watching carefully so the butter doesn't burn. Drop the gnocchi into the sage butter and lightly brown on both sides, tossing often, about 3 minutes. Add the peas and lemon zest, toss, and cook just to heat through. Season with salt and pepper.

To serve:

Transfer the gnocchi to a plate or shallow bowl, sprinkle with Parmesan cheese, and serve.

Lobster Mac and Cheese

This was my favorite Mystery Box challenge, and I didn't even win it! When I saw my little brother's tiny feet as the box began to rise, I could not contain my excitement. I had not seen Cooper in almost a year. I didn't know how much taller he had gotten since I'd seen him last, and I couldn't imagine him getting on an airplane to come see me. I was so happy to see him that I almost forgot I had to cook!

When we went into the pantry, everyone had someone to help them strategize—what kind of protein to grab, what flavors would complement each other best—and I had my little brother saying I should get the "orange cheese" (read: processed cheese) and the elbow macaroni, because that's what mac and cheese is to a six-year-old. Because I didn't want to disappoint him, I said "OK," put them in my basket, and then grabbed the proper ingredients to make a more highbrow mac and cheese. My favorite moment, however, was when Cooper was standing in the balcony watching me grate the three cheeses on the cutting board and he said to me, "Courtney! Do it over the bowl—it's faster!" Having him cheer me on and give me some surprisingly good advice really spurred me on. I wanted to make my little brother proud.

=== SERVES 4 ===

Bring a pot of heavily salted water (the water should literally taste like the sea) to a boil. Fill a large bowl with ice and water and set aside. Drive the tip of a strong knife into the lobster's head and finish the chop so the knife is between the eyes (the heel of the knife should be away from the lobster's body). Immediately plunge the lobster into the boiling water and boil until the lobster becomes bright red (it's important to boil the lobster right after killing it because its meat will spoil quickly), 8 to 10 minutes. Using tongs, remove the lobster from the boiling water and place it in the ice bath to stop the cooking. Keep the water at a boil. Once the lobster has cooled, remove the meat from the tail, knuckles, and claws. The tail can be cut vertically,

Recipe continues

Salt

1 (2-pound/900-g) lobster

½ cup (120 ml) heavy cream

½ cup (120 ml) milk

1 cup (100 g) shredded Gruyère cheese

2 cups (160 g) shredded Gouda cheese

½ teaspoon truffle oil

Freshly grated nutmeg

Freshly ground black pepper

1 pound (450 g) orecchiette

2 teaspoons olive oil

Large outer leaves of 4 Brussels sprouts

Freshly grated Parmigiano-Reggiano cheese

and the meat is easily removed, but the claws and knuckles will need to be cracked with a tool (a nutcracker will do nicely). When extracting the meat from the claws, be sure to remove the blade, as it is inedible. Chop the tail and claw meat into bite-size pieces, but keep the knuckle meat separate (it's the most flavorful part, and will be used for garnish). Tie the lobster shells in cheesecloth and return to the boiling water, cover partially, and boil while you make the cheese sauce (you are now infusing the water you will be boiling the pasta in).

In a medium saucepan, heat the cream and milk over medium heat. Just as the mixture comes to a simmer, reduce the heat to low and gradually sprinkle in both cheeses, stirring gently with a wooden spoon in a figure-eight motion. Don't be too forceful, as you want the sauce to thicken evenly, and rushing it will cause it to separate. Once all the cheese is melted and well combined, about 2 minutes, add the truffle oil and the lobster meat (except the knuckle meat), season with nutmeg and pepper, and turn off the heat.

Remove the cheesecloth sachet of shells from the boiling water, add the pasta, and cook according to the package instructions for al dente. Drain.

Meanwhile, in a medium skillet, heat the olive oil over medium heat. Add the Brussels sprout leaves and cook until well browned, about 5 minutes. Transfer to a paper towel–lined plate and sprinkle with salt.

Return the pasta to the pan it was cooked in, add the cheese sauce with the lobster, and toss to coat. Divide the pasta among four plates, taking care to equally distribute the lobster. Top each plate with some of the reserved knuckle meat and the crispy Brussels sprout leaves. Garnish with grated Parmigiano-Reggiano and serve.

Fish Tacos

For the fish

2 (1-pound/450-g) haddock or other white fish, such as cod or halibut fillets

Salt and freshly ground black pepper

1 large shallot, thinly sliced

¼ cup (10 g) fresh cilantro leaves

Zest and juice of 1 lime

1 tablespoon olive oil

For the cabbage slaw

1 small cabbage, cut in half, cored, and very thinly sliced or coarsely shredded on the large holes of a box grater

1 carrot, coarsely shredded

Zest and juice of ½ lime, or to taste

½ teaspoon sugar

½ teaspoon salt, or to taste

For the salsa

3 tomatoes, chopped

1 small red onion, chopped

1 small jalapeño chile, seeded and finely chopped

2 tablespoons chopped fresh cilantro

Zest and juice of ½ lime, or to taste

Salt

This is an adaptation of a recipe from the Football Team Challenge, in which I was team captain. This challenge was my chance to really put my life experience to the test, and I felt very well prepared. When I was growing up, my family had a small business selling pizzas at local festivals, fairs, and block parties. We would make and serve pizzas for up to five hundred guests a day, usually with a line across the fairgrounds. It helped me take some of the pressure off by thinking of this as just another festival. We had the same audience—hungry kids and their parents—and we were serving them healthy food they enjoyed. Although we did not win the challenge, I represented my family that day and I know I made them incredibly proud. Fish tacos have really become so popular in the last few years and they're a great, light way to add a ton of flavor to any summertime outing. If you want to make your tacos a little more authentic, use two corn tortillas to wrap each taco; this will also strengthen them so they hold more of the delicious fillings.

===== MAKES 12 TACOS =====

To make the fish:
Preheat the oven to 350°F (175°C).

Pull out two sheets of parchment paper slightly larger than the length of a baking sheet. Place one of the fillets on one sheet of parchment and season with salt and pepper. Sprinkle with half of the shallot and cilantro and drizzle half of the lime zest, lime juice, and oil on top. Gather the longer edges of the parchment to meet together over the top of the fish. In two small folds, fold the parchment toward the fish. Now take the two open ends and tuck them underneath the packet itself. Repeat with the second fillet on the second sheet of parchment. Place the fish packets side by side on the baking sheet and bake for 20 minutes, or until opaque throughout.

To make the cabbage slaw:
Combine the cabbage and carrot in a medium bowl. In a small bowl, whisk the lime zest and juice with the sugar and salt. Pour over the

cabbage and toss well to coat. Let marinate while you finish the recipe.

To make the salsa:
In a medium bowl, combine the tomatoes, red onion, jalapeño, cilantro, and lime zest and juice. Season with salt and toss.

To make the avocado crema:
In a food processor, combine the avocados and lime juice and season with salt and pepper; process until smooth. Add the sour cream and pulse until incorporated. Transfer to a bowl and garnish with the cilantro.

To assemble the tacos:
Lay the tortillas on the oven racks (they'll still be warm from cooking the fish) and allow them to soften for a minute or two. Transfer the fish packets to a serving platter and unwrap at the table for dramatic effect. Have your diners assemble their tacos as they choose.

For the avocado crema
2 ripe Hass avocados

Juice of ½ lime, or to taste

Salt and freshly ground black pepper

½ cup (120 ml) sour cream or Mexican crema

1 tablespoon chopped fresh cilantro

For the assembly
12 small corn tortillas (or 24, to double up in each taco)

THE DISH:
I had been waiting for the opportunity to be a team captain all season. When the chance finally came, I was really excited. Although our team lost, we worked extremely well together, and I consider that a win. It didn't make it to air, but Chef Elliot told me that I was the best team captain he'd ever seen in the history of the show. That meant so much to me. With his comment, I felt like I had finally proven myself— as a leader and as someone who was a strong teammate.

Seared Salmon with Lemony Israeli Couscous Salad

Prior to *MasterChef*, I had only attempted to fillet a fish maybe twice in my life. But I had watched a ton of fish-filleting videos on YouTube and would also frequent local fish markets, watching the fishmongers with a careful eye. So when we were presented with salmon during a challenge, I knew to use the spine as my guide and to make long strokes with my knife rather than use a sawing method. And because salmon is an oily fish, I knew I needed an acidic element to balance it out, which I accomplished by including both the zest and juice of the lemon in my Israeli couscous salad, which the judges raved about.

It's important to know that Moroccan couscous and Israeli couscous are two totally different ingredients. Moroccan couscous is made of the smallest grains of semolina mixed with droplets of water, pushed through a woven colander by hand, and left to dry in the sun. Israeli couscous, often called pearl couscous, or *ptitim* in Hebrew, is essentially a very small pasta, also made from semolina or sometimes wheat flour; it is extruded from a machine and is prepared as you would pasta.

This was one of my favorite dishes of the season, and it can be easily used to dress up any dinner party or even a regular Tuesday night in. It's become a staple around my table and I hope it will become one around yours.

=== SERVES 4 ===

For the Israeli couscous
Salt

1 cup (150 g) Israeli couscous

1 small English cucumber, quartered and very thinly sliced crosswise

1 small bulb fennel, cored and thinly sliced

3 tablespoons picked fennel fronds

1 shallot, thinly sliced

Zest and juice of 1 lemon

3 tablespoons olive oil

Freshly ground black pepper

For the salmon
4 (6-ounce/170-g) skin-on salmon fillets

Salt and freshly ground black pepper

3 tablespoons olive oil

To make the Israeli couscous:
Bring a pot of salted water to a boil, add the couscous, and cook according to the package directions for al dente, about 7 minutes. Drain and rinse under cold water to bring the couscous to room temperature, about 30 seconds. Transfer to a bowl and add the cucumber, fennel, fennel fronds, shallot, lemon zest and juice, and

Recipe continues

oil. Season with salt and pepper. Set aside to marinate while you make the salmon (or you can make it up to several hours in advance, cover, and marinate in the refrigerator until ready to serve).

To make the salmon:

Season the flesh side of the salmon with salt and pepper. Heat a large skillet over high heat and add the oil. Just as the oil in the pan gets glossy, add the salmon, skin side down. There should be a good amount of sound—don't try to move the fillets, as you want to get a really great sear on the fish, and once you've got it, the fillet will release itself from the pan. Follow the "flip it and kiss it" rule: Cook the fish 90 percent on the skin side, then flip the fillet and leave it just long enough for it to "kiss" the heat of the pan. Let the fillet rest for half as long as it was cooked and serve alongside the couscous salad.

THE DISH:

Truthfully, a bigger fish is easier to fillet than a smaller one. But what took up most of my time wasn't the actual fillet-ing, but scaling the fish to begin with. I'm often asked if I have any regrets about my *MasterChef* experience and the one thing I wish I had done differently is to have gone and watched Chef Ramsay fillet his fish. I still can't believe none of us went to watch his demonstration. I was so worried about finishing my plate on time that I missed out on a once-in-a-lifetime cooking lesson.

Whole Grilled Branzino

Branzino is a beautiful Mediterranean sea bass that is extremely versatile. You can find this fish at many supermarkets, and if you ask your fishmonger, I'm sure he or she will be happy to clean it for you. This is a fun dish to share with friends who aren't squeamish and don't mind eating with their hands. You could even throw a finger-food-only dinner party if you're feeling really brave! Although you can fillet the fish after it has been cooked, it's much more fun to dig in to it whole. I chose to pair the branzino with the clean, crisp flavor of lemon; once you get comfortable with your own cooking style, you can start adding your own twist on the dish, too.

===== SERVES 2 =====

To make the branzino:

Preheat a cast-iron grill pan over high heat. Pat the fish dry with a paper towel and season the skin with salt and pepper. Stuff the cavities of the fish evenly with the shallot, lemon, and parsley sprigs. Spray the pan with cooking spray and heat until smoke just begins to rise. Add the fish, lower the heat to medium, and cook for about 6 minutes, then flip and cook for another 6 minutes, or until browned and crisp and just cooked through. Transfer the branzino to a serving plate. Meanwhile, prepare the sauce.

To make the sauce:

While the fish is cooking, in a medium saucepan, combine the shallot, lemon, capers, and olives. Place over medium heat and cook until the shallot is softened, about 5 minutes. Add the stock, increase the heat, and reduce by about half, to a sauce consistency. Whisk in the butter and season with salt and pepper.

To serve:

Place the fish whole on a large platter and pour the sauce over the top. Invite your guests to eat with their hands (eating a whole fish with your hands is an easy way to avoid bones, and it makes the meal that much more fun), but offer them utensils if they prefer.

For the branzino

2 (1-pound/450-g) branzini, cleaned (scales, fins, and guts removed)

Salt and freshly ground black pepper

1 small shallot, very thinly sliced

1 lemon, very thinly sliced

2 sprigs fresh parsley

For the sauce

1 small shallot, very thinly sliced

Juice of 1 lemon

2 tablespoons capers

¼ cup (20 g) green olives, pitted and cut in half

1 cup (240 ml) vegetable stock

1 tablespoon unsalted butter

Salt and freshly ground black pepper

Chicken Cordon Bleu

½ cup (50 g) bread crumbs

½ cup (30 g) fresh parsley leaves

1 tablespoon fresh oregano leaves

Salt and cracked black pepper

4 (8-ounce/225-g) boneless, skinless chicken breasts

4 small ham steaks (about 2¼ ounces/65 g and ¼ inch/ 6 mm thick each)

4 slices Swiss cheese (about 8 ounces/225 g total)

1 tablespoon olive oil

For my Sweet Sixteen, my mom and I planned a fancy dinner party. Using Mom's best cookbook, we decided on chicken cordon bleu as the main course, and then she stayed up late pounding out chicken and rolling it with ham and Swiss cheese. My friends showed up in their nice dresses, and my little brothers donned white button-downs and acted as our servers. My brothers actually did a pretty good job and delivered all six courses of my birthday dinner without complaint. Although, looking back now, I think Mom might have bribed them with movie tickets or a new video game. Regardless, I had a memorable Sweet Sixteen, and I was lucky to have spent it with good friends and great food, all facilitated by my wonderful family.

===== SERVES 4 =====

In a food processor, combine the bread crumbs, parsley, oregano, ½ teaspoon salt, and ½ teaspoon pepper and pulse until well combined. Transfer the mixture to a pie plate and set aside.

Lay the chicken breasts between two sheets of plastic wrap and pound them to about ½ inch (1.25 cm) thick. Discard the plastic wrap. Season the top side of the breasts with salt and pepper, top with a ham steak, and follow with a slice of cheese. Carefully roll each breast with the ham and cheese—not as tightly as you would my pork tenderloin (page 143), but more like you were folding a business envelope. Place each roll seam side down on a piece of plastic wrap and wrap very tightly. Refrigerate for 15 to 20 minutes.

Preheat the oven to 350°F (175°C).

Line a baking sheet with parchment paper. Remove the chicken breasts from the refrigerator and remove the plastic wrap. Using a pastry brush or your fingertips, coat the breasts evenly with the olive oil. Place the breasts one at a time into the bread crumb mixture and roll to coat them evenly. Transfer to the baking sheet, seam side down, and bake for 45 minutes, or until the internal temperature reaches 160°F (70°C). Transfer the breasts to a cooling rack to rest for about 5 minutes (while they rest, their temperature will continue to rise to the recommended 165°F/74°C; if you remove the chicken from the oven when the temperature is already at 165°F/74°C, they will wind up overcooked). Serve each breast whole, with a sautéed vegetable of your choice, if you like.

Roast Chicken with Lemon and Olives

1 (4- to 5-pound/1.75- to 2.25-kg) organic chicken

Salt and freshly ground black pepper

3 tablespoons olive oil

2 small fennel bulbs, fronds reserved, cored and cut into 4 wedges each

3 medium yellow onions, cut in half and then into 3 wedges each

2 organic lemons, cut into 8 wedges each and seeds removed

2 sprigs fresh rosemary

10 sprigs fresh thyme

3 Yukon gold potatoes, cut into ¾-inch (2-cm) pieces

½ cup (40 g) pitted green or Kalamata olives

1 tablespoon all-purpose flour

About ¾ cup (180 ml) Simple Chicken Stock (page 104)

My grandma taught me how to truss my first chicken. She grew up on a farm where they raised chickens, so I'm certain she's even plucked one by hand. I remember standing in her kitchen making the chicken "dance" in the sink after stuffing it with lemons and herbs, and her teaching me to tuck its wings and tie its legs together. Afterward we'd take the neck and giblets and make a delicious stock that we used to make soup (I highly recommend doing this for the Italian Wedding Soup on page 105). Learning in Grandma's kitchen, using the equipment she'd had all her life, and sharing that time with her are memories I will cherish forever. Now every time I roast a chicken, I get to relive those incredible experiences and the combination of food and love that will always come to mind for me.

Note: While the vegetables inside the bird's cavity are perfectly fine to eat, their main purpose is to flavor the bird. I choose to leave them stuffed inside the cavity and include them along with the bones when I make my stock (page 104).

======================== SERVES 4 ========================

Preheat the oven to 450°F (230°C).

Place the chicken on a large cutting board. Tie the legs together using kitchen string and tuck the wings behind the back. Season the cavity with 1 teaspoon salt and ½ teaspoon pepper. Season the body with another 1 teaspoon salt and ½ teaspoon pepper, and rub 1 tablespoon of the oil all over the chicken. Place a few fennel, onion, and lemon wedges inside the cavity (as many as will fit snugly), along with a sprig of rosemary and half of the thyme.

In a flameproof roasting pan, combine the remaining fennel, onion, and lemon wedges, the potatoes, olives, and the remaining

Recipe continues

rosemary and thyme and toss with the remaining 2 tablespoons oil. Season with salt and pepper. Set the chicken, breast side up, on top of the vegetables.

Roast the chicken for about 1¼ hours, until an instant-read thermometer inserted into the thickest part of the thigh reads 155°F (70°C)—the temperature will continue to rise as the chicken rests—and the juices run clear when pierced with the thermometer where the thigh and body connect. Tilt the chicken downward so any released juices come out, then transfer the chicken from the roasting pan to a carving board, tent loosely with aluminum foil, and let rest while you prepare the gravy. Remove the vegetables from the pan to a serving bowl (do your best to remove the herb sprigs, but it's okay if some remain) and tent them with foil as well.

Place the roasting pan directly on the stovetop over medium heat. Add the flour and stir with a wooden spoon until the juices are soaked up and the flour is thickened and bubbling. Pour in the chicken stock and scrape the bottom of the pan to release any browned bits; cook, stirring constantly, for about 3 minutes, until a gravy is formed. Add more chicken stock if needed to reach your desired consistency. Transfer to a sauceboat or small bowl.

When ready to serve, remove the kitchen twine and carve the chicken. Serve with the vegetables and the gravy boat passed at the table.

Sumac Duck Breasts with Spring Vegetables and Farro

I remember how nervous I was: It was the *MasterChef* Finale. I had dreamed of this moment, I had watched the incredible cooks before me compete, and I had fought a long, hard battle to get where I was. My appetizer had gone very well, and I was confident I could do a repeat performance with my entrée. I chose duck—the most unforgiving and difficult protein. One minute undercooked and it's purple; one minute overcooked and it's gray, so I felt the pressure mounting for perfect execution. Something that I had learned in the years of watching Chef Ramsay cook on television and from reading his books is that duck needs to begin in a cold pan; that precious duck fat needs to be rendered slowly. The trick with duck is a bit like the trick with fish—it cooks 90 percent skin side down, then you just "flip it and kiss it" to heat it through.

I felt strangely calm during the hour I had to prepare this dish. I was the most proud of this dish, and Chef Elliot said it was the prettiest plate I had presented to him in the entire competition. When you prepare this recipe, it's a good idea to have three pans working at once. It won't be overwhelming; the farro itself takes just about an hour, and the sauce can't be finished until the duck is done. If you follow the instructions and manage your time wisely, all of the components will finish at the same time and you can sit down to enjoy them with a glass of wine and some good company.

—— SERVES 4 ——

To make the pickled chive scapes:
Place the chive scapes in shallow bowl. In a small saucepan, combine the vinegar, peppercorns, sugar, and salt and bring to a boil. Pour the vinegar mixture over the chive scapes and set aside to pickle while you continue with the recipe.

Recipe continues

For the pickled chive scapes
16 chive scapes, trimmed to 2 inches (5 cm) with tops

½ cup (120 ml) champagne vinegar

1 teaspoon green peppercorns

¼ cup (50 g) sugar

¼ teaspoon salt

For the farro
4 cups (1 L) Simple Chicken Stock (page 104)

1 cup (165 g) farro

For the sumac duck breasts
4 duck breasts

4 teaspoons sumac

Salt and freshly ground black pepper

For the vegetables
2 tablespoons olive oil

8 morels, cleaned and cut in half lengthwise

Salt and freshly ground black pepper

1 sprig fresh thyme

2 bulbs green garlic, sliced

Ingredients continue

To make the farro:

In a medium saucepan, bring the chicken stock to a simmer; reduce the heat and keep the stock just below a simmer.

Heat a medium sauté pan over medium heat. Add the farro and cook, stirring, until aromatic, a shade darker, and the grains start to jump from the pan. Ladle ½ cup (120 ml) of the stock into the farro, stirring constantly. When almost all of the stock is absorbed, add another ½ cup (120 ml). Continue adding stock in this manner, stirring constantly, until all of the stock has been incorporated and the farro is cooked through but still al dente, about 1 hour.

While the farro is cooking, make the sumac duck breasts:

Score the duck breasts in a crisscross pattern through the fat but not into the skin. On the flesh side only (as the sumac may burn from the sear), sprinkle the sumac evenly and season with salt and pepper.

Place the duck, skin side down, in a large unheated sauté pan. Turn the heat to medium and cook for 10 to 12 minutes, carefully pouring the rendered fat from the pan into a heatproof container a couple of times as it starts to accumulate. When the fat is rendered as close to the meat as possible—you'll know they are ready when you can no longer see the fat and the skin is almost touching the meat—flip the breasts and cook for about 2 minutes for medium-rare. Leave about 1 tablespoon fat in the pan (you'll use it to make the sauce). Transfer the breasts to a cutting board and let rest while you continue with the recipe.

While the farro and duck are cooking, make the vegetables:

Heat the oil in a large sauté pan. Add the morels, season lightly with salt and pepper, and cook until lightly colored, about 3 minutes. Transfer to a plate. Add the thyme, green garlic, leek, and scallions and cook, stirring, until softened, about 2 minutes. Add the turnips

Recipe continues

½ leek, white and light green parts, sliced

2 scallions, sliced

4 baby turnips, trimmed and quartered

8 Thumbelina or young carrots, trimmed and cut in half

¼ cup (35 g) fresh peas

For the sauce

1 shallot, quartered

2 cloves garlic, smashed

1 sprig fresh rosemary

1 sprig fresh thyme

1 tablespoon brandy

1 cup (240 ml) chicken demi-glace

Juice of ½ lemon

1 tablespoon unsalted butter

Salt and freshly ground black pepper

For the pea "dust"

3 tablespoons dry-roasted peas (or substitute wasabi peas)

Pea tendrils, for garnish

and carrots, cut side down, and cook for about 3 minutes, until nicely colored on the underside; turn and cook for another 3 minutes, or until browned on the second side. Stir in the peas and cook for about 1 minute, until warmed through. Season with salt and pepper and toss the mixed vegetables with the cooked farro; reserve the morels.

To make the sauce:

Using the same pan the duck fat was rendered in, add the shallot, garlic, rosemary, and thyme to the reserved 1 tablespoon fat and cook for 2 minutes. Add the brandy and cook for about 2 minutes, until the alcohol is cooked out. Add the demi-glace and lemon juice, increase the heat to medium-high, and cook until reduced to a thin sauce consistency, about 5 minutes. Strain into a small saucepan or heatproof bowl, whisk in the butter, and season with salt and pepper.

To make the pea "dust":

Place the dried peas in a spice grinder or food processor and process to a powder. Pour through a fine-mesh sieve into a small bowl.

To serve:

Spoon a little sauce onto the center of a plate and arrange about ¾ cup of the vegetables and farro over the sauce. Trim off the ends of each duck breast and slice each breast into 7 pieces; set on top of the farro. Place the morels snugly around the duck. Garnish with pickled scapes and pea tendrils. With your fingertips, sprinkle the dust around the plate in small piles and serve.

Chili con Colby

This recipe comes from a strange request my brother Colby made when I was visiting him for Thanksgiving. I asked him what he wanted with his turkey, and he said chili. I've gotten past the point of being surprised at the requests my brother comes up with, but there is no room for chili in Thanksgiving dinner, so I politely declined. I did, however, write this chili recipe for him so he could make it any time of the year. It's simple enough that he can cook up a large pot of it to share with his friends on Game Day, and of course it's garnished with Colby cheese, because otherwise he probably wouldn't eat it.

3 slices thick-cut bacon, cut into 1-inch (2.5-cm) pieces

1 medium yellow onion, diced

8 ounces (225 g) ground beef

Salt

2 cloves garlic, minced

1 green bell pepper, cored and diced

¼ teaspoon ground cumin

¼ teaspoon ground cayenne

1 (7-ounce/200-g) can chipotle chiles in adobo sauce, chopped

1 (15-ounce/425-g) can black beans, drained and rinsed

1 (15-ounce/425-g) can kidney beans, drained and rinsed

¼ cup (50 g) brown sugar

1 (15-ounce/425-g) can crushed San Marzano tomatoes

1 cup (100 g) shredded Colby cheese

=== SERVES 6 ===

Place the bacon in a large saucepan. Place over medium heat and cook until the bacon fat is rendered, about 5 minutes. Add the onion and cook until translucent, about 5 minutes. Add the ground beef, breaking it up with a wooden spoon, and season generously with salt. Add the garlic and green peppers and cook until the peppers are softened, about 5 minutes. Add the cumin, cayenne, and chipotles and their adobo sauce and stir to combine. Add the black beans, kidney beans, brown sugar, and crushed tomatoes. Stir well, bring to a simmer, then reduce the heat to low and simmer for 30 minutes. Spoon into bowls, top with the cheese, and serve.

Here's me and Colby after I prepared Thanksgiving dinner for him—no chili, but he's not complaining!

Meat Loaf with Haricots Verts and Sweet Potato Mash

For the meat loaf

2 pounds (900 g) mixed ground beef, pork, and veal (any ratio)

1 small yellow onion, minced

1 tablespoon Worcestershire sauce

2 large eggs

3 tablespoons ketchup

2 tablespoons whole milk

½ teaspoon salt, or to taste

½ teaspoon cracked black pepper, or to taste

¼ cup (25 g) bread crumbs

2 tablespoons brown sugar

For the sweet potato mash

2 large sweet potatoes, peeled and cubed

2 tablespoons unsalted butter

¼ cup (60 ml) milk

Salt and freshly ground black pepper

This is my ultimate comfort food. Whenever I'm having a bad day or it's gray and gloomy outside, there's nothing that makes me feel better faster than meat loaf. You may remember how excited I got when Chef Elliot's ground beef dish turned out to be meat loaf—it really is one of my favorites. I remember calling my grandma once to ask for her recipe, and when I told her I was making a one-pound meat loaf—just big enough for me—she nearly fell over laughing. Having six kids and fourteen grandchildren, my sweet grandma just couldn't fathom what "meat loaf for one" would look like. Although I didn't have to make a meat loaf in the first elimination challenge, had I had the chance, this is the one I would have made.

=== SERVES 4 TO 6 ===

To make the meat loaf:

Preheat the oven to 350°F (175°C).

In a large bowl, combine the ground beef, pork, and veal, the onion, Worcestershire sauce, eggs, 1 tablespoon of the ketchup, the milk, salt, and pepper. Using your hands, mix thoroughly, making sure to evenly distribute all the ingredients. Sprinkle the bread crumbs over the top and mix once again. Test your seasoning by cooking a tablespoon of the meat loaf in a hot pan and tasting it; adjust the seasonings if necessary.

Transfer the mixture to a casserole dish or a parchment-lined baking sheet and form it into a 9-by-5-inch (23-by-13-cm) loaf. You can also bake it in a loaf pan, but I prefer a free-form meat loaf because you'll get color on all sides of the meat loaf, as opposed to just the top, and more space in the pan also means you can easily make a delicious pan sauce from the juices released during cooking, should you choose to.

In a small bowl, mix the remaining 2 tablespoons ketchup with the brown sugar. Spread the mixture evenly over the top of the meat loaf and bake for 60 minutes, or until the meat loaf is deeply browned and the juices that have released are bubbling rapidly. Remove from the oven, place the pan on a cooling rack, and let rest for 10 minutes.

To make the sweet potato mash:

While the meat loaf is in the oven, place the sweet potatoes in a large saucepan, add water to cover, and bring to a boil. Cook until fork-tender, 15 to 20 minutes; drain. Return the sweet potatoes to the pot, add the butter and milk, and season with salt and pepper. Using a potato masher or a fork, mash to your desired consistency.

To make the haricots verts:

Toast the hazelnuts in a medium skillet over medium heat until they are lightly browned and you can smell their oils being released. Transfer to a paper towel–lined plate. Add the butter to the pan, and just as it is melted, add the haricots verts and sauté until they are bright green and still have a bit of a crunch when you bite into them, about 3 minutes. Season with salt and pepper.

To serve:

Slice the meat loaf, place a slice on each plate, and serve with the haricots verts and sweet potato mash alongside.

For the haricots verts

¼ cup (35 g) hazelnuts, chopped

2 tablespoons butter

12 ounces (340 g) haricots verts, ends trimmed

Salt and freshly ground black pepper

Not My Mom's Beef Stroganoff

2 (8-ounce/225-g) New York strip steaks (about 1½ inches/4 cm) thick

Salt and freshly ground black pepper

2 tablespoons olive oil

3 ounces (85 g) chanterelle mushrooms, sliced

3 ounces (85 g) cremini mushrooms, sliced

3 ounces (85 g) shiitake mushrooms, stemmed and sliced

1 small yellow onion, diced

2 tablespoons all-purpose flour

1½ cups (360 ml) beef broth

¼ cup (60 ml) heavy cream

1 tablespoon grainy mustard

1 pound (450 g) cooked egg noodles

Fresh parsley leaves, for garnish

When I was testing this recipe, I sent a picture of it to my mom and said, "Look!—I made beef Stroganoff!" Her reply was, "That doesn't look like my beef Stroganoff." Which made me think, she's right—this is *my* beef Stroganoff. And that's how this recipe got its name.

Growing up, it wasn't often that we would all sit down to dinner together, but the rare times we did enjoy a meal together, Mom would often make her beef Stroganoff. This dish has stood out for me for so long because I associate it with family time, and also because it was my introduction to cooking with fresh mushrooms. I learned that you want the mushrooms to be in the pan before anything else, otherwise they won't brown. I've called for chanterelle, cremini, and shiitake mushrooms, but feel free to try the recipe with any variety.

Stroganoff is typically made with cubed beef, but I've elevated this recipe by serving a delicious New York strip steak on top of the mushroom ragù. If you want to get really fancy, I dare you to make your own noodles.

Now that we're older and most of us have moved out of our parents' house, it's even more difficult to get my family in the same room for dinner—or the same state, for that matter—but that doesn't mean I can't try to bribe them with this recipe.

SERVES 4

Season the steak generously with salt and pepper. Heat a large skillet over high heat for about 3 minutes, until very hot. Add 1 tablespoon of the oil, then add the steaks and cook for 4 minutes without moving them to give them a good sear. Turn the steaks and cook for another 4 minutes, or until seared on the second side. Transfer to a cutting board and let rest for 5 minutes.

While the steak is cooking and resting, heat the remaining 1 table-spoon oil in a large skillet over medium-high heat. Add all the mushrooms and sauté until softened, 3 to 4 minutes. Add the onion and cook until translucent, about 2 minutes. Add the flour and stir to coat, about 1 minute. Pour in the broth and cook, stirring to release any stuck bits from the bottom of the pan, until thickened, about 3 minutes. Lower the heat to medium, add the cream and mustard, season with salt and pepper, and cook for about 1 minute, until thickened.

Thinly slice the steaks against the grain. Divide the noodles among four plates, top with the mushroom sauce, and arrange the steak slices over the sauce. Finish with a sprinkling of parsley leaves.

Sorry, Mom—I love you, but this is my beef stroganoff!

Red Wine Beef Stew

2 pounds (900 g) beef shoulder, cut into 1½-inch (4-cm) pieces

Salt and freshly ground black pepper

¼ cup (60 ml) olive oil

4 medium onions, sliced ¼ inch (6 mm) thick

6 fresh thyme sprigs

2 bay leaves

1 small bunch fresh parsley, plus additional leaves for garnish

2 tablespoons all-purpose flour

1 cup (240 ml) pinot noir

6 medium carrots, cut into 1-inch (2.5-cm) pieces

2 medium russet potatoes, peeled and cut into 1-inch (2.5-cm) pieces

1 large clove garlic, smashed

Crusty bread, for serving (optional)

Based loosely on beef bourguignon, this is a simple dish to make for a fall or winter family night. It's hearty and filling and tastes even better after stewing in the fridge overnight, so it only gets better as leftovers. Traditional beef bourguignon is made with mushrooms and pearl onions, but pearl onions are annoying to peel, and I don't particularly like how they taste. I added extra carrots and potatoes in lieu of the mushrooms, which I omitted purely because I'm not partial to the texture mushrooms take on after stewing. Though it is of course absolutely delicious, I decided to stray from some longer braised bourguignon recipes and to create a recipe that could be completed in tandem with a busy schedule.

SERVES 6

Season the beef generously with salt and pepper. Heat the oil in a Dutch oven over high heat. Add half of the beef and sear it to get good color on all sides, about 5 minutes total. Transfer the meat to a plate and repeat with the remaining beef, adding it to the plate as it's done. Add the onions to the oil in the pan, reduce the heat to medium, and cook for about 10 minutes, stirring occasionally, until translucent.

While the onions are cooking, in a 12-inch (30-cm) piece of cheesecloth, tie together the thyme, bay leaves, and parsley.

Add the flour to the onions and stir to coat well; cook for 2 minutes to cook out the starchy flavor. Increase the heat to high, add the pinot noir, and bring to a boil, stirring to release any browned bits from the bottom of the pan. Return the meat to the pan and add the carrots, potatoes, garlic, and cheesecloth-wrapped herbs. Pour 3 cups (720 ml) water into the pot, bring to a simmer, then reduce the heat to low, cover, and simmer for 2 hours. Taste the seasonings and adjust with salt and pepper, if necessary. Spoon into bowls and garnish with a few parsley leaves. Serve with crusty bread, if you like.

Apple-Stuffed Pork Tenderloin with Autumn Slaw and Swiss Chard

This is the dish that won me my second Mystery Box challenge. I remember that day so well, because I had gotten letters from my mom and baby brother, Cooper. Living in Philly has made it difficult to be there for important events in his life, and being away on *MasterChef* for three months had made it that much harder. So when I lifted the Mystery Box to find apples falling around me, I felt so happy. That's because at the end of the street where my parents live, there is a factory that produces applesauce from locally grown apples, and one of Cooper's favorite things to do is to go on bike rides to the "applesauce factory" and back. Seeing those apples and thinking of my brother gave me the extra rush of adrenaline to really attack that Mystery Box. I made a point of using one apple of each variety from the box—I knew that Granny Smiths would hold up the best while cooking, Red Delicious would be excellent raw, and Pink Ladies would offer the most juice. I also made sure to use the entire apple, peel and all. I aimed to show this ingredient the respect it deserved.

Tip: When peeling celeriac, cut a sliver off the bottom so the root is level and stands on its own. Going at it with a vegetable peeler would be tedious and unrewarding; instead, using a sharp knife, cut the skin off in strips from top to bottom like you would a pineapple.

SERVES 4

To make the apple-stuffed pork tenderloin:
First, make the crust: Peel the Granny Smith apple and chop the peels. Core the apple and thinly slice it, reserving the slices. Combine the bread crumbs, pecans, chopped apple peel, cilantro, rosemary, and salt in a food processor and pulse until uniformly broken down into a coarse, sandlike texture. Transfer to a large plate and set aside.

Recipe continues

For the apple-stuffed pork tenderloin

1 small Granny Smith apple

½ cup (50 g) bread crumbs

½ cup (45 g) pecan halves

1 cup (40 g) chopped fresh cilantro leaves and stems

Leaves from 2 (4-inch/10-cm) sprigs fresh rosemary

¼ teaspoon salt, plus more as needed

1 pound (450 g) pork tenderloin

Freshly ground black pepper

¼ cup (30 g) grated Gouda cheese

4 fresh sage leaves, julienned

8 thin slices pancetta

1 tablespoon olive oil

For the slaw

1 small Red Delicious apple

1 small Granny Smith apple

About ½ small celeriac, peeled and cut into matchsticks (about 1 cup/75 g) (see Tip)

Ingredients continue

2 tablespoons apple juice

1 tablespoon fresh lemon juice

Salt and freshly ground black
pepper

1 bunch Swiss chard

1 tablespoon olive oil

2 ounces (55 g) pancetta, diced

1 Honeycrisp apple, cored,
peeled, and diced

¼ cup (60 ml) apple juice

1 teaspoon sugar

1 tablespoon grated lemon zest

2 tablespoons fresh lemon
juice

Salt and freshly ground black
pepper

3 Pink Lady apples, juiced
(about 1½ cups/360 ml juice)

3 tablespoons roughly
chopped peeled fresh ginger

1 stick cinnamon

2 tablespoons unsalted butter

Trim off excess fat and sinew from the tenderloin. Using a meat pounder, pound the whole tenderloin into an approximately 9-by-5-inch (23-by-13-cm) rectangle. Lay the tenderloin flat on a sheet of plastic wrap and season with salt and pepper on both sides. Add a single layer of reserved Granny Smith apple slices on top of the tenderloin, leaving a little space at the edges, then follow with the shredded cheese and sage leaves and finish with the pancetta slices. Starting at the end closest to you, roll the tenderloin away from you, pulling it toward you as you roll to make it tight and keep the filling from falling out (use the plastic wrap to help you roll the tenderloin snugly). Wrap the plastic wrap firmly to secure the shape of the roll and refrigerate for at least 15 minutes or up to a day ahead of cooking.

Preheat the oven to 375°F (190°C).

Remove the stuffed tenderloin from the plastic and rub the oil all around it. Roll the tenderloin onto the bread crumb mixture, pressing it firmly to form a thick crust all around the pork. Place the tenderloin on a baking sheet and bake for about 45 minutes, rotating the baking sheet halfway through cooking, until the internal temperature of the meat reaches 140°F (60°C) (take the temperature by inserting the thermometer into one of the ends of the tenderloin, reaching halfway through to the center of the tenderloin; the temperature will rise a few degrees as it rests). Remove from the oven, tent loosely with foil, and let rest while you continue with the recipe.

To make the slaw:
While the tenderloin is in the oven, peel the Red Delicious and Granny Smith apples and reserve the peels to use for the applesauce. Core the apples and cut them into matchsticks. In a large bowl, combine the apples and celeriac. Add the apple juice and lemon juice and season with salt and pepper. Set aside.

To make the Swiss chard:
Separate the chard leaves from the stems. Roughly chop the leaves and finely dice the stems. Heat the oil in a large sauté pan over medium-high heat. Add the pancetta and diced chard stems and cook for about 5 minutes, until the pancetta starts to brown and the

Recipe continues

chard stems start to soften. Add the diced Honeycrisp apple and continue to cook for another 5 minutes, or until the apples have started to caramelize. Add the chard leaves, apple juice, sugar, and lemon zest and juice and cook until the chard leaves have wilted and the liquid has been absorbed into the vegetables, 3 to 5 minutes. Season with salt and pepper and keep warm or reheat just before serving.

To make the applesauce:

Combine the Pink Lady apple juice, apple peels (reserved from the apple-celeriac slaw), ginger, and cinnamon in a small saucepan, place over medium-high heat, and bring to a high simmer. Continue to simmer until the mixture has reduced and thickened almost to a syrup, about 15 minutes. Strain through a fine-mesh sieve into a clean pan and discard the solids; return to the heat and cook until reduced to a syrup (about ¼ cup/60 ml), another 5 minutes or so. Whisk in the butter and keep warm until you're ready to serve.

To serve:

Slice the stuffed pork tenderloins into 12 medallions. Place about 1 tablespoon of sauce on the center of each of four plates and top each with 3 medallions. Place some slaw on one side of each plate and some chard on the opposite side and serve.

THE DISH:

When we lifted our Mystery Boxes for this challenge and those apples came crashing down, I actually shrieked. I was in the front row, so I had no warning about what was going to happen. I was totally taken by surprise. I said to Chef Ramsay that nothing up until that point in the competition had made me feel as homesick as seeing all those apples. Trust me, they know how to pull your heartstrings! I thought of my grandmother's house with an apple tree in the yard. In the end, it helped me cook my heart out.

Mulled Cider

Mulled cider is something my mom would make from Halloween to Christmas. It made the house smell so good and we could never get enough of it. I came up with the recipe by thinking back to how my mom would make her classic version, then making it my own by adding some of my favorite spices. This recipe has proven time and again to be a hit at holiday parties. Just remember: The longer it simmers, the more intense the flavors get!

===== **SERVES 8 TO 10, with enough for seconds** =====

In a large saucepan, combine the cloves, peppercorns, allspice, and cinnamon and toast over medium heat for about 2 minutes, until aromatic. Add the cider and orange slices, increase the heat to high, and bring to a boil. Reduce the heat to low, cover, and cook at a bare simmer for 1 hour. Ladle straight from the pan into mugs; serve with fresh orange slices and cinnamon sticks and top with a sprinkle of nutmeg.

2 teaspoons whole cloves

½ teaspoon whole black peppercorns

1 tablespoon whole allspice berries

3 cinnamon sticks

1 gallon (3.75 L) apple cider

1 orange, sliced into rounds

Orange slices, cinnamon sticks, and freshly grated nutmeg, for garnish

Casual Friday Dinner and a Movie

Growing up in a family of five kids, we didn't go out to eat very often. We spent our Friday nights with delicious food and a good movie. We would invite friends to join us, and once they smelled the simmering oranges and apple cider along with all the savory scents escaping from the kitchen, we knew they'd never want to go home. Prepare the dishes on this menu—you can even make it a potluck—and then pile onto the couch with blankets and pillows (or make a fort!) and sip your cider for the rest of the evening.

CHAPTER 4

THE RECIPES

There is always room—and time—for dessert.

Give me a sweet pastry or a small confection any day and it's sure to make me smile. For the entirety of my childhood, my mom was the source of my knowledge of dessert. She made all of our family's birthday cakes, despite the fact that she never had the proper equipment. Her resourcefulness taught me to make the best of every situation.

Whenever I've had a long or particularly tough day, there's nothing that makes me feel better than creaming some butter and sugar together with a few eggs and maybe even some heavy cream. Whether I'm making a raspberry pie or cupcakes, I find it therapeutic to measure out the ingredients and get a little bit of flour on my countertop. I'm filled with joy when I look down at the finished product—a towering smokestack or a decadent pavlova—almost too pretty to eat. I hope that when you make my recipes, you will feel the same way and perhaps be inspired to imagine yourself at a fancy pastry shop or finishing off a meal at a five-star restaurant. I also hope that, like me, after staring down at your sweet creations for a moment, you pick up your spoon and dig right in!

Mom's Smokestacks

For the chocolate wafers

¾ cup (100 g) all-purpose flour

⅓ cup plus 1 tablespoon (40 g) cocoa powder

½ cup plus 1 tablespoon (115 g) sugar

⅛ teaspoon salt

⅛ teaspoon baking soda

6½ tablespoons (100 g) unsalted butter, cut into ½-inch (1.25-cm) cubes, chilled

1½ tablespoons milk

½ teaspoon vanilla extract

For the filling

4 cups (1 L) heavy cream

1 teaspoon vanilla extract

This recipe has been a part of my mom's family for generations. She calls them "Grandma's smokestacks," but I call them Mom's. They're supposed to be made from packaged chocolate wafers, but I decided to create my own wafer recipe to give this dessert a bit of an upgrade. Don't worry; I asked Mom's permission first. The key to this recipe is letting the smokestacks sit overnight so the whipped cream can soften the chocolate wafers and absorb the sugar from them. If you don't let them sit overnight, you'll get crunchy wafers and bland whipped cream, so be patient and you will be rewarded!

═══ MAKES 6 SMOKESTACKS (32 chocolate wafers) ═══

To make the chocolate wafers:
Preheat the oven to 350°F (175°C).

Combine the flour, cocoa powder, sugar, salt, and baking soda in a food processor and pulse to combine. Add the butter and process until the mixture resembles cornmeal. With the food processor still running, pour in the milk and vanilla and process just until the dough comes together.

Place the dough onto a lightly floured surface and form it into a log measuring 1¼ inches (3 cm) in diameter and 8 inches (20 cm) long. Wrap the shaped dough in plastic wrap and chill in the refrigerator for 1 hour.

Line a 9-by-12-inch (23-by-30-cm) baking sheet with parchment paper. After the dough is chilled, remove the plastic wrap and first score, then cut ¼-inch (6-mm) slices (scoring the dough first will ensure that all of your slices are the same width), placing them on the parchment about 1 inch (2.5 cm) apart. Bake for 8 to 10 minutes, then remove from the oven and let cool on a wire rack (the wafers will be very soft, so instead of using a spatula to transfer each wafer from the sheet to the rack, gently slide the entire parchment off the

Recipe continues

baking sheet and onto the cooling rack). You will have three batches of wafers to bake. As each batch is baking, rewrap the remaining dough and keep it in the refrigerator. The wafers should crisp as they cool; if they haven't crisped, they may have been cut too thick or not baked long enough, and it's okay to put them back into the oven for a few minutes more.

To make the filling:

In the bowl of a stand mixer fitted with the wire whisk, combine the heavy cream and vanilla. Whip at high speed until the cream forms stiff peaks. Spoon the mixture into a pastry bag fitted with a medium star tip. Store the whipped cream in the refrigerator until the wafers have cooled completely.

To assemble:

Start with one chocolate wafer and squeeze the whipped cream in a circle large enough to cover the wafer. Layer with another wafer. Press each wafer down gently, but not so much that the whipped cream squeezes out the sides. Continue in this fashion until you have used 5 chocolate wafers. At the top of the fifth wafer, make a much smaller circle of whipped cream. After completing all of the stacks, you should have one or two wafers remaining. Crumble the additional 2 wafers and sprinkle as a garnish over the top of each smokestack. Place the smokestacks in a covered container and let them sit in the refrigerator overnight. As they rest, the whipped cream will absorb the sweetness of the wafers and the wafers will become soft. You will be able to eat these with a spoon.

Aunt Karen's Chocolate Chip Cookies

My aunt Karen made the greatest chocolate chip cookies I've ever eaten. They were so delicious that in sixth grade I entered them into a baking contest. They were crunchy and slightly chewy and could stand up to big glasses of milk without crumbling. After Aunt Karen passed away, there weren't too many people who had her recipe, so it was only at holidays that my cousin Emily would dig out her mom's recipe and make us a huge batch as a gift. I am very lucky to have Aunt Karen's memory live on in this recipe, because what better way can you show someone you love them than with a batch of warm homemade chocolate chip cookies?

Note: Aunt Karen never used butter in her cookies. To keep her recipe authentic, I chose not to include butter either. If you would prefer to use butter instead of shortening, it can be substituted one for one (by volume, not weight), or you could try half shortening and half butter. But then they wouldn't be Aunt Karen's!

4½ cups (550 g) all-purpose flour

2 teaspoons salt

1 teaspoon baking soda

2 cups (385 g) vegetable shortening

2 cups (400 g) granulated sugar

1 cup (220 g) brown sugar

2 teaspoons vanilla extract

4 large eggs

8 ounces (225 g) semisweet chocolate chips

MAKES 4 DOZEN COOKIES

Preheat the oven to 350°F (175°C). Line a baking sheet with parchment paper.

In a large bowl, whisk together the flour, salt, and baking soda.

In the bowl of a stand mixer fitted with the paddle attachment, beat the shortening, both sugars, and the vanilla on high speed until light and fluffy, about 2 minutes. Add the eggs one at a time and beat on medium-high speed until they are incorporated, about 1 minute. Reduce the mixer speed to low and add the dry ingredients in three portions, mixing the dough only until each addition is incorporated and scraping down the insides of the bowl between additions. Add the chocolate chips and mix until just combined.

Drop heaping tablespoons (or use an ice cream scooper) of dough about 2 inches (5 cm) apart on the prepared baking sheet. Bake for 8 to 12 minutes, until golden brown. Transfer the baking sheet to a cooling rack and let the cookies rest for 10 to 15 minutes before eating.

Linzer Cookies

2¼ cups (285 g) all-purpose flour

1¼ cups (170 g) nuts (hazelnuts or almonds, or a combination)

1½ teaspoons ground cinnamon

¼ teaspoon salt

1 cup (2 sticks/225 g) unsalted butter, softened

⅔ cup (130 g) granulated sugar

1 teaspoon vanilla extract

Zest of 1 lemon

½ cup (150 g) raspberry or apricot preserves

¼ cup (32 g) confectioners' sugar

My favorite coffee shop in the world is Java's in Rochester, New York. The walls are covered floor to ceiling with incredible pieces of art, and there is a grand piano in the center of the shop adorned with wildflowers. In the evening, silent movies are played on a projection screen, and the food is seriously delicious. I spent my eighteenth birthday at Java's with my closest friends, sipping foamy chai, nibbling heart-shaped linzer cookies filled with raspberry preserves, and talking about which colleges we were going to apply to. Now every time I'm back home for a visit, I make a point of visiting Java's for those amazing cookies; in between trips, I'll whip up a batch of these whenever I want to be transported back there.

MAKES 24 COOKIES

Combine the flour, nuts, cinnamon, and salt in a food processor and process, stopping to scrape the inside edge and bottom of the bowl a few times, until the nuts are finely ground into the flour. In the bowl of a stand mixer fitted with the paddle attachment, combine the butter, granulated sugar, vanilla, and lemon zest and beat on medium speed until smooth and well combined, about 1 minute. Reduce the mixer speed to low and add the nut-flour mixture in three batches, beating just until the dough begins to clump together, about 1 minute.

Turn the dough onto a sheet of plastic wrap, and, using your hands, press the dough together to form a flat round disk about ¾ inch (2 cm) thick. Cover the dough with another layer of plastic wrap and refrigerate for at least 30 minutes or up to 2 days.

Preheat the oven to 350°F (175°C).

Remove the dough from the refrigerator and allow it to soften a bit but still be firm enough to roll and handle, anywhere from 5 to 15 minutes depending on your kitchen temperature. Roll out half of the dough ¼ inch (6 mm) thick. Using the rim of a glass or a cookie cutter, cut out as many cookies as you can, dipping the cookie cutter into flour as necessary to prevent sticking. If at any point the dough becomes too soft to handle, slide it onto a cookie sheet, place it in the refrigerator for a few minutes to firm up, and proceed again. Using a wide, flat metal spatula, transfer the cut cookies to parchment paper–lined baking sheets, placing them 1 inch (2.5 cm) apart. Using a small heart- or diamond-shaped cookie cutter, cut out the center of half of the cookies to make a window. Place in the oven and bake for 15 minutes, or until the edges are light golden brown. Transfer to a cooling rack to cool completely. Repeat with the remaining dough, gently pressing together the scraps to re-roll, being careful not to overwork the dough.

Spread the preserves evenly across the whole cookies and layer a cut-out cookie on top of each. Dust the cookies with confectioners' sugar and serve.

THE DISH:
The honey cake (page 167) had actually been my audition dish. When the time came to make a dessert for the first Mystery Box, I decided to present it to the judges again as my signature dessert—but this time I was making it on the spot, which certainly added some pressure. I specifically remember when Joe tasted the cake and commented on the berry coulis. I was so nervous that I stumbled over my words horribly. He asked how it got so smooth and I told him how I passed it through the chinois— stuttering the whole time. I couldn't believe he was actually talking to me!

Earl Grey Cupcakes with Lemon Glaze and Lavender Cream

These cupcakes were so much fun to create. During the testing process, I shared them with friends and asked what their opinion was (I had to be very discreet, as the final episode had yet to be aired), and nearly everyone responded with amazement and curiosity. "There's something special in there!" they would say, or "It needs to be served at weddings!" What they couldn't put their finger on was the bergamot extract—you know, that citrus flavor that is the trademark of Earl Grey tea. It's not a very common ingredient, but you can find it in specialty stores or online, and when you have it, it will last a long time. Because these cupcakes are "frosted" with a pastry cream, be sure to keep them in a temperature-controlled room or you'll risk the frosting melting.

Note: The batter can also be formed into two 8-inch (20-cm) rounds and the recipe turned into a delicious lemon-glazed, pastry-cream-filled layer cake. Either way, they're a great treat that will add a little glamour to any occasion.

=========== MAKES 24 CUPCAKES ===========

To make the cupcakes:
Preheat the oven to 350°F (175°C) and line two 12-cup cupcake pans.

In the bowl of a stand mixer fitted with the paddle attachment, cream the butter and granulated sugar for about 1 minute. Add the bergamot extract, then the eggs, one at a time. In a separate large bowl, whisk together the flour, salt, baking powder, and baking soda. Incorporate the flour mixture and the milk into the creamed butter mixture in three additions, starting and finishing with the flour mixture. Using a rubber spatula, scrape down the sides of the bowl and beat just until the mixture is uniform. Pour the batter evenly into the cupcake liners and give the pans a good rap on a table to release any

Recipe continues

For the cupcakes

1 cup (2 sticks/225 g) unsalted butter, at room temperature

1½ cups (300 g) granulated sugar

2 teaspoons bergamot extract

3 large eggs

2½ cups (300 g) cake flour, or all-purpose flour sifted twice

½ teaspoon salt

1½ teaspoons baking powder

¼ teaspoon baking soda

1 cup (240 ml) whole milk

For the lavender pastry cream

3 cups (720 ml) whole milk

3 tablespoons dried lavender flowers

8 large egg yolks

1 cup (200 g) granulated sugar

½ cup (70 g) cornstarch

2 tablespoons unsalted butter

For the glaze

4 cups (400 g) confectioners' sugar

Zest and juice of 2 lemons

air bubbles. Smooth the tops of the cupcakes with a metal spatula. Bake for 30 to 35 minutes, until a toothpick inserted into the middle of a cupcake comes out clean. Cool the pans on cooling racks for 10 minutes before inverting to get the cupcakes out of the pans.

To make the lavender pastry cream:

In a small saucepan, combine the milk and lavender flowers and place over medium heat. Meanwhile, in a medium bowl, whisk the egg yolks, granulated sugar, and cornstarch. Once the milk-lavender mixture comes to a boil, pour through a sieve into the egg yolk mixture, pressing against the flowers with a rubber spatula. Set aside the sieve and immediately whisk the mixture. Quickly rinse out the milk saucepan just to remove any lingering lavender flowers, pour the milk mixture back into the saucepan, return to the heat, and whisk vigorously until thick. Remove from the heat, add the butter, and whisk until the pastry cream is uniform. Pour the pastry cream into a metal bowl, cover with plastic wrap directly touching the surface, and allow to cool in the refrigerator for 30 minutes. When you are ready to use the pastry cream, remove it from the refrigerator and place it in a stand mixer fitted with the paddle attachment. Beat the pastry cream for about 30 seconds, until it is smooth and uniform in consistency.

To make the glaze:

In a small bowl, whisk the confectioners' sugar and lemon zest and juice until a glaze forms. Adjust the consistency with a few drops of water if necessary.

To finish the cupcakes:

Dip each cupcake into the lemon glaze, covering the surface evenly, then set aside to let the glaze set up, about 15 minutes. Fit a piping bag with a medium star tip and fill the bag with the lavender pastry cream. Pipe a pastry cream rosette onto the center of each cupcake. The cupcakes will keep for up to 2 days in a covered container in the refrigerator.

Dad's Raspberry Pie

My dad doesn't have too many food preferences; he enjoys spicy chicken wings, sour candies, and coffee. But he does have one favorite, and that is raspberry pie. Since his birthday is in July, which happens to be raspberry season, I make my dad a raspberry pie every year as his present. Raspberry pie is not as easy as you might think. When raspberries cook down, they release a lot of liquid, and when I first started making this recipe I ended up with runny pies. When this happened Mom would turn the pie into a delicious sundae topping to save me from feeling like I had failed miserably.

The first Pressure Test turned out to be blueberry pie, and my mom told me later that she was very concerned for me. What she didn't know was that I had practiced making different types of pie before I left for *MasterChef*. I studied and made this recipe over and over again, and boy, was I proud of the pie I produced. If you struggle in the beginning as I did, it's okay; you can do what Mom did and turn your pie into a sundae topping or blend it into a milkshake. But when you do nail it, you'll be so proud, and the lucky person you make it for will be extremely happy, too.

=== MAKES ONE 9-INCH (23-cm) PIE ===

To make the crust:

In a food processor, combine the flour and salt and pulse to combine. Add the butter and shortening and pulse a few times, until the mixture resembles coarse cornmeal. Add the ice water and pulse again until the mixture just forms a ball. Remove the dough from the machine and divide it in half. Shape the halves into two disks, wrap them in plastic, and refrigerate for at least 20 minutes or up to 1 day.

Remove one disk of the dough from the refrigerator and place it between two sheets of plastic wrap (this eliminates the need for flour and will result in a more tender crust). Roll out the dough to form a 10-inch (25-cm) circle. Remove the top piece of plastic wrap and invert the crust onto a pie plate. Remove the remaining plastic wrap. Roll out the second disk of dough the same way as the first,

For the crust

2½ cups (320 g) all-purpose flour

1 teaspoon salt

½ cup (1 stick/115 g) unsalted butter, cut into ½-inch (1.25-cm) cubes, chilled

½ cup (95 g) vegetable shortening baking stick, cut into cubes, chilled

¼ cup (60 ml) ice water

For the filling

6 cups (3 pints/840 g) fresh raspberries

1½ cups (300 g) sugar

¼ cup (28 g) cornstarch

For the egg wash

1 large egg

⅛ teaspoon salt

Recipe continues

remove the top piece of plastic, and carefully cut the dough into 12 ribbons about ¾ inch (2 cm) wide. Gently transfer the ribbons to a baking sheet and refrigerate them while you make the filling (refrigerating the slices while you prepare the filling prevents them from softening too much and results in a flakier crust).

Preheat the oven to 400°F (200°C).

To make the filling:

Place the raspberries in a large bowl. Sift the sugar and cornstarch into another bowl and add to the raspberries. Toss the berries to coat them evenly and let sit at room temperature to macerate for 10 minutes.

To assemble the lattice top:

Remove the dough ribbons from the refrigerator and allow them to soften for about 5 minutes so you can safely bend them back while you weave the lattice. While the ribbons are softening, scrape the raspberry mixture with its juices into the bottom crust. Lay 6 dough ribbons across the top of the raspberries, and from there, fold back alternating dough pieces to place 6 more ribbons crosswise, alternating the folded-back pieces each time. This will give you the woven lattice. Trim and fold the excess dough onto the rim of the pie plate. To flute the crust, pinch the edges together between your thumb and forefinger at a slight angle around the edges of the pie.

To make the egg wash:

In a small bowl, whisk the egg with the salt. Using a pastry brush, gently brush the egg wash over the lattice and fluted rim of the dough.

To bake the pie:

Bake the pie, uncovered, for 20 minutes, then reduce the oven temperature to 350°F (175°C) and bake for another 45 minutes, or until the filling bubbles and the crust is a uniform golden color without any wet spots on the bottom (which would indicate raw dough). If the crust is browning too quickly, gently cover it with aluminum foil. Remove the pie from the oven and place on a cooling rack. Let the pie cool completely before cutting so the juices can set up, and your pie will slice beautifully. Wrap in plastic wrap and store in the refrigerator for up to 1 week; bring to room temperature when you are ready to eat your pie. The pie can also be frozen, well wrapped in plastic, for up to 2 months.

Honey Cake with Mixed Berry Coulis and Vanilla Whipped Cream

This is the cake that started it all: Adapted from and inspired by Julie Richardson's *Vintage Cakes*, this is the recipe I brought to my casting audition. I walked to the audition with the cake in a picnic basket—along with a vintage plate, cake stand, and fork—and waited more than six hours for my audition group to be called. This is also the recipe that won the first Mystery Box!

Because it is so delicious, this cake does not last long. The secret is in the honey you use. I use wildflower, but you can change the flavor significantly depending on which varietal you use; buckwheat and lavender are also good choices. The coulis adds an important level of acidity; otherwise the whole dish will be too sweet for you to eat more than a few bites. This cake is best served slightly warm, and I love it as a snack served with tea or coffee.

===== SERVES 10 =====

To make the cake:

Preheat the oven to 350°F (175°C). Butter and flour a 9-inch (23-cm) round cake pan.

In a small bowl, whisk together the flour, baking powder, and salt and set aside. In the bowl of a stand mixer fitted with the paddle attachment, beat the butter, sugar, honey, and vanilla for about 3 minutes, until lightened in color. Add the eggs and yolk one at a time and mix until well incorporated, about 2 minutes. Add the flour mixture alternately with the buttermilk and mix just until blended. Pour the batter into the prepared cake pan and bake for 45 to 50 minutes, until the center is firm. The cake will take on a deep golden color from the honey in the batter. Remove the cake from the oven and let it cool slightly, about 10 minutes, then invert the cake onto a large plate.

Recipe continues

For the honey cake

2¼ cups (285 g) all-purpose flour

2 teaspoons baking powder

1 teaspoon salt

¾ cup plus 2 tablespoons (200 g) unsalted butter, at room temperature

¾ cup (150 g) sugar

⅓ cup (113 g) honey

2 teaspoons vanilla extract

2 large eggs

1 large egg yolk

1 cup (240 ml) buttermilk

For the honey caramel topping

½ cup (170 g) honey

¼ cup (50 g) sugar

4 tablespoons (½ stick/55 g) unsalted butter

1½ cups (150 g) pecans, toasted and chopped

Ingredients continue

To make the honey caramel topping:

In a small saucepan, combine the honey, sugar, and butter. Bring to a low simmer and cook for about 8 minutes, until the caramel reaches 230°F (110°C) on a candy thermometer. Remove from the heat and set aside. Using an ⅛-inch (6-mm) dowel or a chopstick, pierce holes through the top of the cake and spoon over half the caramel mixture, spreading it evenly across the top. Next, sprinkle the pecans on top of the caramel. Finish by pouring the remaining caramel over the pecans.

To make the mixed berry coulis:

In a medium saucepan, combine the berries, sugar, cardamom, cinnamon, vanilla bean seeds and pod, brandy, and ¼ cup (60 ml) water. Bring to a low simmer and cook for 15 to 20 minutes, stirring occasionally, until you reach a thick syruplike consistency. Pass the mixture through a fine-mesh sieve into a bowl and set aside.

To make the vanilla whipped cream:

In a large bowl, whisk the cream with the vanilla seeds until the cream forms stiff peaks.

To serve:

Spread a spoonful of berry coulis diagonally on a plate. Place a slice of honey cake on top of the coulis. Garnish with the whipped cream and some honeycomb, if you like. The cake will keep, well wrapped in the refrigerator, for up to 1 week.

For the mixed berry coulis

1½ cups (170 g) fresh raspberries

1½ cups (170 g) fresh blackberries

¼ cup (50 g) sugar

4 cardamom pods, crushed

2 cinnamon sticks

½ vanilla bean, split and scraped

2 tablespoons brandy

For the vanilla whipped cream

1 cup (240 ml) heavy cream

Seeds from ½ vanilla bean

Honeycomb (optional)

Vanilla Cheesecake with Strawberry Coulis

For the crust

⅔ cup (80 g) graham cracker crumbs

⅓ cup (75 g) unsalted butter, melted

3 tablespoons sugar

¼ teaspoon salt

For the filling

20 ounces (570 g) cream cheese, at room temperature

¾ cup (150 g) sugar

½ teaspoon lemon zest

1 tablespoon fresh lemon juice

1 teaspoon vanilla extract

Pinch of salt

2 large eggs

½ cup (120 ml) sour cream

This cheesecake was my ticket to the *MasterChef* Finale, and I will tell you something—the first time I ever made a cheesecake, I made the same mistake that sent Leslie home with his Boston Cream Pie. I was at my grandma's house with my cousin Jessica, and we were making no-bake cheesecake; all we had to do was make the crust and whisk together the filling. My grandma had a big container filled with what I thought was sugar. Oh, lord, it was salt. With the first bite, we looked at one another with confused faces and all simultaneously spit into our napkins. When Chef Ramsay said that every home cook at one time or another makes the mistake of confusing salt for sugar, he certainly had that right.

For this challenge we had to make three different cakes, and having only made cheesecake once before, I knew I had to nail it. A thought came to me that gave me great confidence: You can't make a New York cheesecake without Philadelphia cream cheese. And the rest is history!

MAKES ONE 8-INCH (20-cm) CHEESECAKE

To make the crust:

Preheat the oven to 350°F (175°C). Spray an 8-inch (20-cm) spring-form pan with nonstick cooking spray. Line the pan with a parchment round cut to fit and spray again.

Place the graham cracker crumbs in a food processor. Add the melted butter, the sugar, and salt and pulse to combine. Using your fingers, press the crumb mixture evenly across the bottom and about ½ inch (1.25 cm) up the inside wall of the pan. Bake for 5 minutes, then remove the pan from the oven and place on a cooling rack.

Reduce the oven temperature to 325°F (165°C) for baking the cheesecake.

To prepare the water bath:

In a large saucepan, bring 8 cups (2 L) water to a boil. You may not need this much water, depending on the size of the water bath pan you set your cheesecake into (a roasting pan or a high-sided casserole dish would work well).

To make the filling:

In the bowl of a stand mixer fitted with the paddle attachment, beat the cream cheese on medium speed until fluffy, 1 to 2 minutes. Gradually beat in the sugar 1 tablespoon at a time. Add the lemon zest and juice, the vanilla, and salt and mix to combine. Scrape down the sides of the bowl using a plastic spatula. Beat in the eggs one at a time and continue to scrape down the sides of the bowl after each addition. Beat in the sour cream until the batter is creamy and has a uniform texture, about 1 minute.

Wrap the bottom and three-quarters up the outside of the springform pan in foil, using at least two layers of foil to prevent tears from occurring (tears could allow water to enter the cheesecake). Place the foil-wrapped springform pan in a roasting pan or high-sided casserole dish. Pour the cheesecake filling into the springform pan, smoothing the top evenly with a flat metal spatula. Place the roasting pan with the cheesecake in the oven and pour the prepared boiling water into the roasting pan to come halfway up the sides of the springform pan and create a water bath

Bake until the cake is light golden and the center is set (when you tap the side of the pan, the center just barely moves), about 1 hour. Remove the cheesecake from the oven while still in the roasting pan and place on a heatproof surface. Lift the cheesecake out of the water bath with the foil still intact and place on a cooling rack.

Recipe continues

For the strawberry coulis

2 cups (335 g) whole fresh strawberries , plus ¼ cup (40 g) strawberries, chopped medium small

1 tablespoon sugar

1 tablespoon fresh lemon juice

1 tablespoon cornstarch

Carefully remove the foil wrap and let the cheesecake sit to cool completely on the rack, 1 to 2 hours at room temperature. Place the cheesecake in a sealed container or cover with plastic wrap and refrigerate for at least 6 hours or ideally overnight. When you are ready to remove the cheesecake from the pan, run a small flat metal spatula or knife around the inside edge of the pan, going slowly to keep the crust intact. Unhinge and remove the springform ring. Run a long thin metal spatula or knife under the bottom of the cheese-cake to release it from the pan.

To make the strawberry coulis:

Stem the whole strawberries and put them in a blender. Blend on medium speed until the berries are pureed, about 1 minute (you'll have about 1 cup/240 ml strawberry puree).

In a small saucepan, combine the strawberry puree, sugar, and lemon juice and bring to a simmer over medium heat. In a small bowl, whisk the cornstarch and 1 table-spoon water to make a slurry. Whisking constantly, add the cornstarch slurry and bring to a boil. Strain the mixture through a sieve, cover, and set in the refrigerator to chill. When you are ready to use the coulis, add the chopped fresh strawberries. To serve, slice the cheesecake and garnish by drizzling the coulis over the top of the cake.

Colby and I must be two and three in this photo. During the hot summers, Grandma would drive us out to Red Jacket Orchards where we could pick baskets full of our own strawberries. At the end of the day we would be covered in dirt and straw-berry juice—which meant it was a successful trip.

Cherry Meringues with Salted Chocolate and Spicy Almonds

I remember looking up at my mom on the balcony before the final round of the *MasterChef* Finale and mouthing to her, "This dish is hard." I knew my dessert was going to be the most challenging part of the meal, as I really went out on a limb. But that's what *MasterChef* is all about—big risk, big reward.

I created this dish for a few reasons, a major one being I wanted to show the judges I knew how to apply correction. I made meringues and pastry cream because I had messed them both up in previous challenges, and I wanted to try a more avant-garde plating. However, I was so focused on tasting every component to make sure each one was perfect that I accidentally ate one of the meringues I needed for the judges! Despite that mistake, as the clock began to count down the final ten seconds, I decided to truly enjoy my absolute last time cooking in the *MasterChef* kitchen, knowing that the happiness of that experience was something that no one could take away. As Chef Elliot says, "It's just food," and I did everything I possibly could to show the judges I wasn't going to win this competition playing it safe; I wanted to win by putting my soul on the plate and giving the competition everything I had. This recipe includes all of the corrections I was given from the judges and is plated a little differently.

Note: Cherry syrup can be difficult to find, which is why I made it optional. Also be aware that your serving sizes will vary based on the size of your plating glasses, so keep that in mind as you build your parfait-style dessert.

=== SERVES 10 ===

To make the cherry meringues:
Preheat the oven to 225°F (110°C). Line a baking sheet with parchment paper.

Recipe continues

For the cherry meringues
2 large egg whites, at room temperature

1 teaspoon fresh lemon juice

⅔ cup (130 g) sugar

¼ teaspoon cream of tartar

1 tablespoon cherry syrup (optional)

For the pastry cream
½ cup (100 g) sugar

¼ cup (28 g) cornstarch

4 large egg yolks

1½ cups (360 ml) milk

½ vanilla bean, split and scraped

½ cup (120 ml) sour cream

For the almond crumble
1½ tablespoons (21 g) unsalted butter

¼ cup (50 g) sugar

1 tablespoon (28 g) honey

2 tablespoons (25 g) all-purpose flour

½ cup (120 ml) heavy cream

1¼ cups (125 g) sliced almonds

Ingredients continue

¼ cup (35 g) crystallized ginger

½ teaspoon salt

For the spiced almonds
⅔ cup (100 g) Marcona almonds

6 tablespoons (64 g) confectioners' sugar

1 tablespoon vodka

¾ teaspoon garam masala

For the cherries
½ cup (120 ml) black cherry juice

½ cup (100 g) sugar

¼ cup (60 ml) Chambord

1 tablespoon honey

2 tablespoons fresh lemon juice

1 teaspoon vanilla extract

⅛ teaspoon freshly grated nutmeg

20 fresh black cherries, cut in half and pitted

For the salted chocolate ganache
4 ounces (115 g) dark chocolate, chopped

7 tablespoons (105 ml) heavy cream

1 tablespoon light corn syrup

1 teaspoon Maldon sea salt, or to taste

In the bowl of a stand mixer fitted with the whisk attachment, beat the egg whites on high speed until frothy, then add the lemon juice. When the whites begin to form soft peaks, add the sugar, one-third at a time. Add the cream of tartar and pour the cherry syrup, if using, down the inside of the bowl. Continue whipping the meringue until stiff peaks form. Fit a pastry bag with a ½-inch (1.25-cm) plain tip and fill with the meringue. Pipe the meringue onto the prepared baking sheet, making 20 to 24 rounds approximately 1¾ inches (4.5 cm) in diameter. Each meringue round will have a little pointed tip. Dip your finger in a small bowl of cool water and gently push each tip flat into the meringue round. Bake the meringues for 40 to 45 minutes, until firm to the touch. Remove the meringues from the oven and cool on a cooling rack; they may deflate slightly, which is okay. Increase the oven temperature to 375°F (225°C) for the almond crumble.

To make the pastry cream:
In a large bowl, whisk together the sugar and cornstarch, add the egg yolks, and whisk until the mixture is well blended. In a small saucepan, combine the milk and vanilla bean seeds. Place over medium heat and bring the milk to the scalding point. Remove the vanilla bean, rinse, and set aside to dry for future use. Slowly temper the egg yolk mixture by adding the hot milk in a slow drizzle, whisking constantly. Once incorporated, return the mixture to the saucepan and bring to a bubbling simmer, whisking constantly. Transfer the pastry cream to a bowl, cover with plastic wrap, and chill in the refrigerator until cool, then fold in the sour cream. When you are ready to use the pastry cream, remove it from the refrigerator and place it in the clean bowl of a stand mixer fitted with the paddle attachment. Beat the pastry cream briefly, about 30 seconds, until smooth and uniform in consistency.

To make the almond crumble:
In a medium saucepan, melt the butter over medium heat. Add the sugar and honey and stir to dissolve. Add the flour and cook for about 2 minutes. Add the heavy cream, almonds, ginger, and salt. Stir and continue to cook for 1 minute. Spread the mixture in a thin layer on a baking sheet lined with a nonstick silicone baking mat (if you don't have one, use parchment paper). Bake for 15 to

Recipe continues

20 minutes, until golden. Cool completely, transfer the almonds to a food processor, and pulse to crumble.

To make the spiced almonds:

Combine all the ingredients in a small saucepan. Place over medium heat, stir to combine, and cook until the sugar begins to crystallize; when the nuts are evenly coated in sugar, they are ready. Remove from the pan and cool on a parchment paper–lined baking sheet. When the nuts have cooled completely, give them a coarse chop.

To make the cherries:

In a small saucepan, combine the cherry juice, sugar, Chambord, honey, lemon juice, vanilla, and nutmeg and heat over medium heat. Bring to a simmer and cook for about 15 minutes, until reduced to a syrupy consistency. Toss in the halved cherries and mix. Remove from the heat and place the cherries in the refrigerator to cool.

To make the chocolate ganache:

Place the chocolate in a small heatproof bowl. Put the cream and corn syrup in a small saucepan and bring to a simmer over medium heat. Pour the cream over the chocolate and whisk until smooth and fully melted. Cool to room temperature. You will use the Maldon salt when you assemble the meringue cookies.

To assemble and plate:

Spread 1 tablespoon ganache on the bottom (flat side) of one meringue, sprinkle the ganache with a dash of Maldon salt, and top with another meringue to form a sandwich. Repeat with the rest of the meringues.

Using a ¾ cup (180 ml) wide-mouthed champagne glass, you will build a parfait-style dessert. Spoon or pipe ⅓ cup pastry cream into the bottom. Next, sprinkle 1½ teaspoons of the Marcona almonds on top of the pastry cream. Add 4 cherry halves plus 1 teaspoon of their syrup. Set 1 meringue sandwich cookie on top, and pour another 1½ teaspoons of cherry syrup on top. Sprinkle with 2 teaspoons almond crumble. Serve immediately.

Note: If your glasses are bigger, feel free to add more meringue sandwiches to accommodate.

Basil Pavlovas with Fresh Strawberries and Mint Whipped Cream

This delicious dessert is named after the famous Russian ballerina Anna Pavlova. Anna Pavlova was the first ballerina to ever go on tour and the original dancer of the famous ballet "The Dying Swan." I earned my BFA in dance performance from The University of the Arts, and with this dessert I wanted to pay tribute to the classic art and my first love.

Very much like a ballerina's aesthetic, a Pavlova is light and airy. It is a single large meringue decorated with beautiful fruits and fluffy whipped cream. Sadly, Pavlovas do not hold up well in the refrigerator and must be eaten immediately after they are topped with the whipped cream and fruit, so this isn't a dessert that can be assembled in advance.

It is crucial to whip egg whites in a completely clean bowl; if there is anything in the bowl at all—even the smallest trace of egg yolk—the whites won't stiffen. And I'll share with you a tip from Chef Ramsay: Although many recipes will tell you to begin on medium speed and then add the sugar before moving to high speed, this is wrong. Do not do it. Chef Ramsay says, "You cannot gain momentum by going slowly," so begin your whipping on full speed and you will be successful.

=== SERVES 8 TO 10 ===

To make the meringue:

Line a baking sheet with a piece of parchment paper with a 7-inch (18-cm) circle drawn on the underside (you can trace the rim of a bowl).

Place the egg whites in the bowl of a stand mixer fitted with the whisk attachment.

In a blender, combine the basil with ½ cup (120 ml) water and puree on high speed. Pour into a small saucepan and add ¼ cup (50 g) of the sugar. Bring the mixture to a boil over medium heat and cook for

Recipe continues

For the meringue

4 large egg whites, at room temperature

8 large fresh basil leaves, plus 6 large fresh basil leaves, cut into chiffonade

1¼ cups (250 g) sugar

1 teaspoon white vinegar

2 teaspoons cornstarch

For the fruit topping

1 pint (320 g) fresh strawberries, hulled and sliced

3 tablespoons sugar

1 teaspoon fresh lemon juice

4 large fresh mint leaves, cut into chiffonade

For the mint whipped cream

1 cup (240 ml) heavy cream

¼ teaspoon mint extract

about 12 minutes to reduce it to a syruplike consistency. Pour the syrup through a sieve into a small bowl and set aside. Begin whisking the egg whites on high speed, and when they become frothy, add the basil syrup in a small, steady stream. Next, slowly add the remaining 1 cup (200 g) sugar, 1 tablespoon at a time. Add the vinegar and whip for 10 seconds. Stop the mixer and sift the cornstarch over the egg white mixture. Continue to whip the egg whites until stiff peaks form. Remove the bowl from the mixer and fold in the basil chiffonade.

Preheat the oven to 225°F (110°C).

Using a large spoon, transfer the meringue to the baking sheet, using the drawn circle as a guide. Shape the meringue by using a rubber or metal spatula. Make a slight indentation on the top of the meringue; this is where the filling will sit when you assemble the Pavlova. Place the meringue in the oven and bake for 1 hour (resist the urge to open the oven, as doing so will cause the Pavlova to deflate and ruin it). Turn the oven off and leave the meringue in the oven for 2 hours, or until it has cooled completely. Remove the meringue from the oven and begin to prepare the fruit and whipped cream.

To make the fruit topping:
In a small bowl, combine the sliced strawberries, sugar, lemon juice, and mint chiffonade. Place in the refrigerator and allow the fruit topping to macerate for at least 30 minutes and up to 2 hours.

To make the mint whipped cream:
In the bowl of a stand mixer fitted with the whisk attachment, whip the heavy cream and mint extract until soft peaks form.

To assemble the Pavlova:
Transfer the cooled meringue to a serving plate and spoon the whipped cream in a soft pile on top of the meringue. With a slotted spoon, place the strawberry topping on top of the whipped cream in an even layer. Drizzle the remaining juices over the top of the Pavlova, allowing them to trickle down the sides of the meringue. Serve immediately.

Grandma's Fried Dough

¾ cup (150 g) granulated sugar

2 tablespoons ground cinnamon

1 recipe pizza dough (see page 106)

Vegetable oil, for frying

Confectioners' sugar, ground cinnamon, and/or freshly grated nutmeg, for garnish (optional)

At carnivals they're called elephant ears, doughboys, or flying saucers, but at our stand, it's called fried dough. When I was growing up, our family would sell dough and mini pizzas at festivals and fairs; the stand was run by the whole family, and while the grownups worked, my grandpa would barter with the carnival workers for free rides for the grandkids.

My grandpa turned ninety-two this year, and he's still working the stand; I've finally realized what he means when he says "Come get them while they're hot! This week we're real fast, last week we were half-fast!" (Get it?) Tossed in a simple mix of sugar and cinnamon, these fried doughs make me think of summertime and family. As I mentioned in the pizza recipe (page 106), for an authentic Lapresi meal, you can use the second half of your pizza dough to make fried dough for dessert.

===== MAKES 8 FRIED DOUGHS =====

In a medium bowl, whisk the granulated sugar and cinnamon until well combined. Spread over a large plate and set aside.

Using a knife, divide the pizza dough in half, then cut each half into 4 equal pieces. Using your hands (more of the pads of your hands than your fingertips), stretch the pieces out into rectangles 8 inches (20 cm) long by ⅛ inch (3 mm). It's best to focus on stretching the dough wider first; otherwise you'll have long skinny doughs that might not fit into your pan. Start in the middle of the dough and work your way toward the edges; do your best not to allow holes to appear, but if some do, it's okay.

Add enough oil to come ½ inch (1.25 cm) up the sides of a large sauté pan. Place the pan over medium-high heat and heat the oil until a candy thermometer reads 350°F (175°C). Two pieces at a time, gently lay the dough into the oil (away from your body so if it splashes it doesn't splash on you) and fry until the edges just start to brown (it's okay if the middles are only lightly colored), 2 to 3 minutes. Using tongs, flip the dough (again, away from your body) and fry until the edges start to brown on the second side, another 2 to 3 minutes. Remove the dough from the oil, letting excess oil drip back into the pan, and place directly onto the cinnamon sugar; toss it well to coat. Repeat with the remaining dough, cooking two pieces at a time and tossing with the cinnamon sugar as they are done. Sprinkle with confectioners' sugar, cinnamon, and/or nutmeg if you choose. Serve immediately.

Here I am working in the famous fried dough stand I enjoyed helping out at every festival and I learned how to stretch and sugar the doughs. Grandma always said we could eat as many as we wanted, and sometimes we took her up on the offer, heading home with bellyaches. The best part of working at the summertime festivals was watching Fourth of July fireworks with a fried dough in my hand.

Avocado Sorbetto

4 medium Hass avocados,
cut in half, pitted, and flesh
scooped out

½ cup (100 g) sugar

Toasted almond slices, for
garnish (optional)

Seriously—don't knock it till you've tried it. This is the most incredible sorbetto I have ever eaten. I wrote this book for the people I love, and wouldn't you know it, some of them are vegan. So this one's for them.

Because there isn't any milk, cream, or other form of liquid in this recipe, this sorbetto will not melt like you might expect. It will stay firm longer and won't get watery, making it perfect for sweltering days. Avocados are so creamy, rich, and delicious—not to mention good for you—how could you pass up a slowly churned, lightly sweetened frozen avocado treat? The recipe is very simple to double or triple, so you can easily serve a large group this elegant treat!

=========================== SERVES 4 ===========================

In a food processor, combine the avocado flesh and sugar and process, scraping the sides of the machine once or twice as needed, until the mixture is smooth and the sugar granules have dissolved into the avocado (taste it to check), about 2 minutes.

Using a rubber spatula, transfer the mixture to an ice cream maker and churn according to the manufacturer's instructions. If you don't have an ice cream machine, transfer to a shallow freezer-safe pan; place the pan in the freezer for 1 hour, then stir the mixture with an electric mixer or a sturdy spoon, breaking up any large chunks and aerating the soon-to-be sorbetto. Repeat once more, and, using a rubber spatula, transfer the now sorbetto into an airtight container and freeze until ready to serve. Scoop into bowls and serve, garnished with toasted almond slices, if you like.

Croquembouche

For the egg wash

1 large egg

For the pâte à choux

½ cup (1 stick/115 g) unsalted butter

1½ tablespoons sugar

¾ teaspoon salt

1¼ cups (160 g) all-purpose flour

5 large eggs

For the pastry cream

½ cup (100 g) sugar

⅓ cup (42 g) cornstarch

4 large egg yolks

1½ teaspoons vanilla extract

2 cups (480 ml) whole milk

¼ teaspoon salt

2 tablespoons unsalted butter, at room temperature

For the caramel

3 cups (600 g) sugar

¼ teaspoon cream of tartar

This dessert—which literally means "crunches in the mouth"—had me crunching under pressure in the most difficult *MasterChef* Pressure Test I participated in. I had never made a croquembouche before, but my mom often talked about them and about how the fancy ones would be covered in spun sugar. I was really proud of Mom when she made a croquembouche for my sister Colette's Sweet Sixteen and showered her tower with sugar from a fork. Mom didn't have the high-end culinary tools she needed to make the difficult decorations, but she was resourceful and always made it work, and I brought her high standards with me into the *MasterChef* kitchen.

When the judges announced we would be making croquembouche, I was scared, but I knew that if I could pull this off, my mom would be so proud of me. At this point in the competition, I was facing some tough competitors. I actually almost admitted defeat to Chef Ramsay when I told him I thought I could be going home, but instead I just kept repeating to myself, "This is where it counts. This is your chance to change your life." I put my head down and focused so intensely, and after time was called and I looked at my croquembouche, I was filled with such joy and pride I didn't even care that I had spun sugar all over my Louboutins!

So I guess the moral of the story is that you can only fail when you've given up on yourself. I saw myself slipping, and made a comeback that I am truly proud of.

SERVES 8 TO 10

Preheat the oven to 425° F (220°C). Line two baking sheets with parchment paper.

To make the egg wash:
In a small bowl, beat together the egg and ½ teaspoon water and set aside.

To make the pâte à choux batter:

In a medium saucepan, combine 1¼ cups (300 ml) water, the butter, sugar, and salt. Bring to a boil, stirring with a wooden spoon until the butter is completely melted. Add the flour all at once and beat vigorously, cooking the dough over medium heat until it is dried out and holds together in a mass in the center of the pan, 2 to 4 minutes. Transfer the batter to the bowl of a stand mixer fitted with the paddle attachment. Mix on low speed for 1 minute to cool the batter. Add the eggs one at a time on medium-low speed, mixing completely between additions and scraping down the sides of the bowl. The batter is done when it is smooth and shiny and drops from a spatula in a slow, wide ribbon.

Pipe 25 puffs onto each of the prepared baking sheets, each puff about 1½ inches (4 cm) in diameter. Using a pastry brush, gently brush egg wash over each puff, tapping down the small tip on top of each puff as you brush them. Put the sheets in the oven and lower the temperature to 400°F (200°C). Bake for 30 to 40 minutes, until the puffs are browned on the bottom and sound hollow when tapped (although resist the urge to open the oven, because loss of heat would cause the puffs to deflate). Turn the heat off and leave in the oven for an additional 10 minutes to ensure that they are crisp. Remove from the oven, place the sheet on a cooling rack, and cool completely before filling.

To make the pastry cream:

In a medium bowl, whisk together the sugar and cornstarch. Add the egg yolks and vanilla and whisk until the mixture is well blended. In a medium saucepan, combine the milk and salt; place over medium heat and bring to the scalding point. Slowly temper the egg mixture by adding the hot milk in a slow drizzle, whisking constantly. Return the egg-and-milk mixture to the pan, increase the heat to medium-high, and cook, whisking constantly, until thick bubbles burst on the

Recipe continues

surface. Stir in the butter until it is melted and the pastry cream is smooth and uniform. Transfer the pastry cream to a bowl and cover with plastic wrap directly touching the surface of the cream so a skin does not form. Place in the refrigerator to cool.

When you are ready to use the pastry cream, remove it from the refrigerator and place it in the bowl of a stand mixer fitted with the paddle attachment. Beat the pastry cream briefly, about 30 seconds, until it is smooth and uniform in consistency.

Holding the puffs gently, pierce the bottom of each puff with a small round pastry tip, then fit a pastry bag with a ¼-inch (6-mm) round pastry tip. Fill the bag with the pastry cream and fill each puff. You will feel the puffs swell when the pastry cream is added.

To make the caramel:
In a small heavy-bottomed saucepan, combine the sugar and cream of tartar. Pour ½ cup (120 ml) water over the sugar. Do not stir (if you stir it, it will crystallize the sugar and the caramel won't form). Heat the mixture over medium-low heat until the sugar dissolves, cleaning any sugar crystals off the inside of the pan with a wet pastry brush, if needed. Raise the heat to medium-high, bring to a boil, and boil until the sugar turns light caramel in color and the temperature reads 300°F to 305°F (150°C to 152°C) on a candy thermometer (still without stirring). Shock the bottom of the pan in ice water to stop the caramel from further cooking (otherwise it will harden to a point where it is no longer usable), then place the caramel over a pot of boiling water to keep it warm and liquefied while you continue working

To assemble the croquembouche:
Using a flat glass plate with a 12-inch (30-cm) diameter, you will assemble a tower of cream puffs, sticking them together with the caramel. Always be cautious when working with caramel, because it is so very hot!

Recipe continues

Holding a filled cream puff carefully, dip the bottom in the caramel and stick the caramel side onto the plate. Continue placing individual cream puffs in a circle to fit the base of your plate (see photo 1 on page 186). It's a good idea to space the puffs out first before dipping them in the caramel in case you need to rearrange. Continue in this method, changing to dipping the sides of the cream puffs, and arranging your second circle of puffs on top of the first circle with the rounded sides facing out. As you're making each circle, you want to stagger the cream puffs so there are no gaps in your tower (see photo 2 on page 186), and as you build your tower upward you will decrease the number of puffs with each new circle. It is helpful to use the larger puffs on the lower circles and the smaller ones in the upper circles. You can look down at the tower of puffs from above to help perceive and maintain a symmetrical cone shape. As you finish placing the cream puffs the tower should lean together so that you can have a single cream puff atop (see photo 3 on page 186).

To make the spun sugar:

Using a cut-off whisk if you have one (if you don't, use a fork rather than a regular whisk, as a regular whisk will not give you the desired effect), working quickly, dip the tips of the whisk in the remaining caramel and flick the whisk back and forth horizontally, vertically, and in a circle around the croquembouche (see photo 4 on page 186). Repeatedly dip the whisk and continue flicking the caramel to create fine threads of spun sugar around the croquembouche.

To serve:

Have your guests pluck the puffs off of the croquembouche as they like. At some point, the tower will fall, which is part of the fun of eating a croquembouche!

Chocolate-Covered Pretzels

16 ounces (455 g) milk chocolate melting wafers

12 ounces (340 g) salted pretzel sticks

Sprinkles, edible glitter, or chopped nuts, for garnish

These simple treats are easy to make but have a ton of flavor and are a favorite everywhere I take them. My entire childhood, Mom always gave them out as gifts or party favors and brought them to different gatherings. In addition to pretzels, she would dip Pringles potato chips, strawberries, and (gasp) even peanut butter crackers in chocolate! Make a small batch for yourself or a larger batch to share with your friends. These delicious, decorated bites go to show that even the simplest things can be beautiful and decadent!

MAKES 32 PRETZELS

Create a double boiler by filling a medium saucepan halfway with water and placing a heatproof bowl on top of, but not touching, the water in the pan. Bring the water to a simmer. Add the chocolate to the bowl and, stirring frequently, melt the chocolate. Once the chocolate has melted, remove the bowl from the pan (carefully, because the bowl will be hot) and pour the melted chocolate into a shallow baking dish. Working quickly, place the pretzel sticks in the melted chocolate. With a fork, roll the pretzel sticks so the chocolate covers all sides. Remove the pretzels and lay them to cool on a sheet of parchment paper. If you want to add garnishes, do so before the chocolate has hardened.

Garam Masala Hot Chocolate

When testing and perfecting the cherry meringues recipe (page 173), I had some leftover garam masala. Just for fun, I got a little experimental and swirled it into my hot chocolate. I loved it! The Middle Eastern spices are so versatile that they can stand up to both sweet and savory applications. This drink will taste even better swirled with a chocolate-covered pretzel, and it is a perfect sweet treat for after dinner. If you really want to wow, double the recipe and serve it at your next dinner party instead of coffee.

3 cups (720 ml) whole milk

1½ cups (360 ml) heavy cream

¼ teaspoon salt

1½ cups (275 g) dark chocolate chips (preferably 70% cacao)

1 teaspoon garam masala

2 teaspoons sugar

=== SERVES 4 ===

In a medium saucepan, combine the milk, 1 cup (240 ml) of the cream, and the salt. Place over medium-low heat and bring just to a simmer. Add half of the chocolate chips and stir with a heatproof spatula until the chocolate chips are melted. Add the garam masala, sugar, and the remaining chocolate chips and stir until all of the chips are melted. Remove from the heat and give the mixture a few good whisks to fully incorporate the ingredients.

To make the whipped cream, pour the remaining ½ cup (120 ml) cream into a Mason jar or other jar with a tight-fitting lid and shake until you can't feel the cream moving around anymore and you're holding a jar of whipped cream, 1 to 2 minutes.

Divide the hot chocolate among four mugs and top with the whipped cream.

Dessert Social

Have a decadent evening get-together by hosting a dessert social. Ask each of your friends to dress up and bring their favorite dessert wine while you decorate the table with an array of homemade treats that your guests can nibble on throughout the evening. Light a bunch of candles of all shapes and sizes, play some classical music, and then finish the night lounging in your fancy clothes, sipping this spicy hot chocolate out of antique teacups. This "sweet hour" will be one for the books.

Acknowledgments

Never in my wildest dreams would I have imagined writing a book, and now that it's finished, I almost can't believe I did it. There are so many people I would like to thank from the bottom of my heart for making this the most wonderful experience of my life.

First, I would like to thank God. It is through Him that all things are possible.

To my family: Mom, Dad, Colby, Connor, Colette, and Cooper. Without you guys, I wouldn't be the person I am today. You will never know how much you all inspire me and how much I love you. I won this competition for you, and I filled this book with our memories. Mom, you WILL get your dream kitchen one day, I swear it. Daddy, thank you for telling me that I am worthy. Sometimes when life gets tough, we believe that we don't deserve the best, and I am grateful that you have always reminded me otherwise. Colby and Connor, hearing you both coach me during the finale was the most empowering and supportive thing you could have done. I love you both so much. Colette, I am so proud of the young lady you are growing up to be! If my time on *Master Chef* teaches you anything, I hope that it is to stay true to yourself and to always give 110%. And to Cooper, thank you for being the biggest joy in our lives! It melts my heart with happiness to watch you cook and to hear you say you want to be a chef like me.

To my wonderful grandparents—Tom, Shirley, Beverly, and Mickey— who have always supported me, from my first dance recital to the

MasterChef Finale. Thank you for being a source of inspiration and love; all I ever want to do is to make you proud.

To my friends:

Christina Wilson: You told me that fate loves the fearless, and you never doubted me. From ballet competitions to culinary competitions, thank you for being my biggest source of encouragement.

To Gunnar Clark: I wouldn't have made it past day one without your help—thank you!

Karina and Justin Mitchell: I wouldn't have submitted my application on time without you both; thank you for being such wonderful friends.

Rosie Stovall: Thank you for encouraging me to follow through with my audition—you knew how nervous I was.

Dave Notartomaso: Thank you for being a confidant, and a valuable resource during this process. I am very grateful.

Scott Megill: Thank you for letting me into your kitchen not knowing me from a can of paint. You've taught me so much.

My neighbor Laura Clinton: Thank you for taking care of my cat while I was away filming. I'm sure he was also grateful.

Alejandra Carillon: Thank you for sneaking that good luck note in my suitcase during the top 100 in LA—I looked at it often during the competition.

To my publicist and friend, Sara Kelly: Thank you for making it your personal goal to see me as happy and successful as possible. Thank you for being on call at all hours of the day and night to answer my thousands of questions—and for encouraging me to truly enjoy this experience.

To Abby and Katie of Smak Parlour: Thank you for being my personal stylists for the past six years. I am so happy I got to represent Smak while on the show.

To my Stepping Stones Family: Thank you for encouraging me to continually raise the bar, and for insisting that one day you would see me on national television. I am so happy that I lived up to your prediction and made you so proud.

To my many, many friends, thank you SO much for not begging, prying and trying to "figure out" the outcome. I am so thankful.

To Jennifer May, Erin McDowell, Barb Fritz, and their assistants: Thank you for three beautiful days of shooting the photographs for this book. You captured my dishes perfectly. Thank you for your attention to detail, respect toward my personal and sentimental props, and for bringing my recipes to life. I could not have asked for a better photographer, food, or prop stylist.

To Leda Scheintab, Nash Patel, and Patricia Austin: The friendship we all have created is irreplaceable and I am so thankful to have the three of you in my life. Thank you for welcoming me into your homes and helping me test out (and taste—Nash!!) each and every one of the recipes. I will never forget how we had to test the recipes in complete secrecy, high on a mountaintop, in beautiful Vermont. From nicknaming me Coco, to making me wear pants and T-shirts, you all helped me to remain incognito. Leda, you have been the most patient, kind, and giving person, thank you for guiding me to make this book the best it can be. Patricia, I will forever remember the day we foraged golden chanterelles and climbed a mountain together. You have so much knowledge to give, and are the most talented and passionate baker I know.

To the incredible judges, Chef Gordon Ramsay, Chef Graham Elliot, and Mr. Joe Bastianich: I am still in complete awe and amazement that I got to work under your expert direction. Having the three of you as my mentors is worth more than any prize. Knowing that I—as your student—surpassed your expectations and made the leap from home cook to be recognized as an aspiring chef is my greatest accomplishment. I am forever grateful for every compliment, critique, and bit of encouragement and praise you have ever sent my way. I look up to the three of you with such immense respect; I can only hope to continue to learn from you for the remainder of my career.

To Samantha Weiner, Danielle Young, and the team at ABRAMS: Without you, this book is just a collection of recipes. I appreciate and value the time and effort to build, organize, and design my book. Thank you for being patient when I missed deadlines, got writer's block, or was just plain overwhelmed.

To the incredible and insanely talented Christian Louboutin. You have said that "A shoe has so much more to offer than just to walk" and I am honored to have competed and won in your magnificent works of art. I can only imagine that one day, I will get to prepare you a glorious dinner.

To Chef Sandee Birdsong, Chef Avery Pursell, Whitney Webster, and the entire Culinary Team: You went above and beyond the call of duty every single day. Thank you for encouraging my culinary aspirations and for teaching me so much. Your passion for our success was truly evident and I am so grateful for the times you lent listening ears and shoulders to cry on when the competition got tough, and the homesickness set in.

Thank you to our awesome cast wranglers, aka our personal assistants: JP, you are awesome. Chris,

I had the most fun touring around Hollywood Boulevard and going into ALL of the wax museums with you. To Anthony, Mikey, CJ, Joel, and Maika: thank you for carting us around in the giant van. Thank you to Bob the Medic for being fully prepared with Band-Aids, and to the stylists Christina, Hilda, and Laura for making us always look our best.

To my amazing story producer, Tommy Rasera: You were the unseen face I spoke to in every interview and I am THRILLED about the friendship we've created. From the first apron, to the actual trophy—I am so happy to have shared it with you.

To the talented director, Brian "the voice from above" Smith, and the gorgeous Viking, Anna Moulaison-Moore, and Brady Hess, our behind-the-scenes assistant director. To the incredible production team: Yasmin Shackleton, Robin Ashbrook, and Adeline Ramage Rooney. Suzy Beck: I looked forward to hearing you read the rules for every challenge giving you jazz hands every day. Scott Hanlon from sound: Thank you for being in charge of having my voice be heard.

Thank you to my friends Scottish Francis, Elise Mayfield, Cutter Brewer, Jaimee Vitolo, Tyler Viars, and all my other fellow *MasterChef* contestants for challenging me to compete to the best of my ability. I wish you all the best in your future, and am certain that you have an incredible life with food ahead of you.

A big thank you to the team at ShineAmerica, Triple7PR, OnePotatoTwoPotato, FOX, and ABRAMS, specifically Joe Schlosser, Julie Holland, Vivi Zigler, Monica Austin, Edwin Karapetian, Eden Gaha, Paul Franklin, Rob Hughes, Yvonne Bennett, Ivana Zbozinek, Thomas Ferguson, Elizabeth Lockwood, Krista Armentrout, Franc Roddam, Simon Andreae, Melissa Gold, and Armando Solares.

Resources

DiBruno Brothers
www.dibruno.com
215-665-9220
*Quark, cheeses, sweetbreads,
pigs ears' and other meats, duck fat,
bergamot extract*

Fante's Kitchen Shop
www.fantes.com
800-44-FANTE
*Spices, sugars, natural flavors,
extracts, oils, and kitchen utensils*

Kalustyan's
www.kalustyans.com
800-352-3451
*Herbs and spices, sugars, natural flavors,
crystallized ginger, culinary lavender
flowers, rosewater, extracts*

Nuts.com
www.nuts.com
800-558-6887
*Marcona almonds, dried fruits, herbs
and spices*

OliveNation
www.olivenation.com
781-989-2033
*Culinary lavender flowers, rosewater,
extracts, and baking ingredients*

The Spice House
www.thespicehouse.com
847-328-3711
*Bergamot extract, herbs and spices,
seasonings*

Tea Trekker
www.teatrekker.com
413-584-5116
Genmaicha and other quality teas

Zamouri Spices
www.zamourispices.com
913-829-5988
*Rosebud petals, crystalized ginger,
herbs and spices, seasonings*

Index